BETWEEN US

*A True Story of Longing for
Love and Letters*

Pirkko Rytkonen

ENDORSEMENTS

"A sweet and unforgettable story about the longings of the heart. *Between Us* is the true story of a girl and a boy who lived across the ocean from each other, became pen pals, and searched for a way to make their dreams come true in this poignant, true, and well written story of yearnings and doubts." Susy Flory, New York Times bestselling author and co-author of 16 books, director of a writers conference, and founder of Everything Memoir

"*Between Us* captivates the heart in a symphony of love letters between strangers across an ocean. A young Finnish seminary student wished to connect with a pen pal in Canada who could teach him English. Sometimes a girl must take a chance even when common sense tells her not to. Unforgettable true story." Penelope Childers, Award-Winning Author of *My Promise to Alex*

"Pirkko shares a love story that spans over the seas and over the years. A true testimony of what it means to live by faith. An inspirational tale that shares how God leads us if we pray and wait patiently for His plan." Kimberley Payne, author of *Through Trials to Triumph: A Memoir of a Catholic Girl's High School Years*

"In *Between Us*, Pirkko introduces us to her young self, an insecure immigrant woman who is navigating through the difficult life questions we all face. Where do I belong? What is my purpose? Will I find someone to love? In this honest memoir, Pirkko reveals her heart to us through vivid storytelling and authentic original letters in which she shares her fears and struggles, hopes and dreams. Anyone who has lived the immigrant experience or has suffered through a long-distance relationship will connect deeply with this story. I believe the strongest message in the book is that love heals all wounds. This true love story is a testimony and a tribute to the power of love and faith." Anita Fisher, Pastoral Staff, Faith City Church, Thunder Bay

"*Between Us* is a story of love with a mutual faith between two different worlds. Pirkko couldn't have foreseen a forever future with a mission-minded young man. Even the ocean could not separate what was meant to be. The author recounts life adventures that were stored away in a box for decades. This is not your typical love story." Anita Ball, Author of *Box of Shame: A Memoir of Addiction, Survival, and Forgiveness*

"Pirkko Rytkonen shares not only the beginnings of a decades-long love story but also those things that could have hindered it from ever unfolding. Honest. Vulnerable. And overflowing with hope. I highly recommend *Between Us,* Antti and Pirkko's story of shared love—for one another and for the Lord who brought them together." Steph Beth Nickel — Editor

"Pirkko's story is filled with romance and intrigue with unusual twists and turns. It's a story of challenges and dreams, love and hope. I couldn't put it down." Linda Greenberg

"In this beautiful and poignant love story, the author draws us in very close to her journey of faith and love with God and her beloved partner in life. One takes away a deep understanding of what unconditional love is, and that love truly conquers all, including our insecurities and questions when we journey with God. This testament to true love is a compelling and delightful read. Enjoy!" Miriam Kemppainen, Pastor, Saalem/Bayview Family Church, Toronto

AUTHOR'S NOTE

THE PERSONAL LETTERS we exchanged as pen pals started out in English, but as the relationship developed into soulmate status, and later evolved into dating, we wrote in Finnish. Therefore, the letters are loosely translated into English from the original text. To shorten the text, I included mostly excerpts from the correspondence and made minimal wording changes to help with readability. The correspondence lasted for three years, from June 1970 to June 1973, and such, the memoir is based on a short time period from our early twenties, and comprised of topics, people, and culture we discussed. Some people's names have been changed as well as some details to protect others' privacy. Conversations are constructed from the actual letters, but others are created from my memory to the best of my knowledge. To be authentic, I used details and facts from the letters compressed into short quotes.

DEDICATION

To my husband, Antti…
Thank you for your love and patience in our journey…
Happy 50th wedding anniversary to us!

1

looking for adventure

A KNOCK AT the front door prompted me to hurry. I'd dreamt about this adventure and worked hard to make it happen, and now it'd arrived.

Books neatly placed on the bookshelves reminded me of school, but this summer would be different. I might never sleep in my narrow single bed or sit at this desk again.

A streak of morning sunshine burst through the window as I imagined what life would be like in Finland. The green leaves on the shrubbery in front of our house swayed like the thoughts in my head. I zipped my carry-on bag and snapped the blue suitcase shut while mixed feelings crisscrossed in my head. For the first time, I feared the future that I'd cultivated in my thoughts and the idea of living away from friends and family. *Would I miss them too much?*

"Aren't you ready? Sofia is at the door waiting!" Dad's heavy footsteps approached the front door, coming closer so I could hear him without yelling.

"Just wait. I'm coming." I shook my head. If he wanted me to hurry, why didn't he pick up my suitcase by the door?

My mom, dad, brother, and sister, along with my friend and I, all piled into the black Chevy Impala. Dad ignited the engine. One last look at the house, just in case. I made these plans on my own and wanted others to bless them, but no words of encouragement came. Was I running away or looking for adventure? With my flight bag and purse pressing on my lap, I breathed a sigh of relief. We were off!

My hometown of Thunder Bay, located in Northwestern Ontario, the middle of Canada, north of Minnesota, had a population of approximately 100,000. The demographics included immigrants from many European countries, with people of Finnish heritage being the largest group at about 10,000 people.

Emigration from Finland had begun in the early nineteenth century as workers looked for better economic opportunities. This was the case for my family of eight, which included six children ranging from age nine years to nine months. In 1960, we arrived in Montreal, Canada with only a few suitcases and a lot of hope and faith that life would be better. Now, after only eight years, I wanted to search for my self-identity and independence. We considered Finland the old country, a place of birth, but where did I belong, really? My parents had made the choice for me so far. Now, at seventeen, I yearned to learn more about my background, to discover my roots, and hopefully, myself. *Who am I?*

My family, like all other Finnish immigrants, lived comfortably in the Finnish cultural environment, where people easily conversed in their own language at stores, restaurants, banks, and churches, and even took part in theatrical productions and sports teams. The famous Bay Street, dedicated to Finnish businesses, held prominence in the city. As a result, many Finnish immigrants did not need to learn English, as most men worked in the forest and mining industries, and mothers stayed home with the kids, and they could conduct business in their own language.

On weekends I worked as a waitress at a restaurant owned and operated by a strong Finnish woman. This was where I met many people of my background, including young adults who came to Canada for better opportunities in life. My cultural experience included communicating in the Finnish language with the patrons, who were mostly young single men, but staff and students from the university also frequented the diner. The men worked out of town at the bush camps or mines and lived in small apartments or rooming houses and ate their meals in the Finnish restaurants, which all served home-cooked meals. Some came every day just to flirt with the pretty workers. I served customers with a smile and friendly conversation in both languages. The owner preferred Christian employees, and we often invited customers to church to hear the gospel in Finnish. The choices: Pentecostal, Free, Lutheran, or Baptist.

The menu featured a mixture of Canadian and Finnish foods made from scratch and served in large portions. T-bone Steak with mashed potatoes, gravy, and vegetables was the most expensive item on the menu, a real pleaser for hungry men. The restaurant served breakfast foods like bacon and eggs as well, any time of day, but the thin Finnish pancakes with strawberries topped with whipped cream sold like hotcakes.

The famous *mojakka*, a hearty stew made with stewing beef or fish, also served men's appetites well. No one around town knew where the word *mojakka* came from since it's not understood in Finland and is better known as *lihakeitto* there. My boss added heaping mounds of roast beef, potatoes, carrots, celery, onions, butter, and flour for thickening with just enough black pepper and salt to the *mojakka*. Another stew was the *kalakeitto,* which included lake trout, potatoes, carrots, celery, and milk-thickened flour, seasoned with salt and pepper. Though it had its fishy stink, my sense of disdain for the meal didn't distract me like the pungent fish stench of my father's fish frying at home.

The restaurant owner was known for her fabulous cooking skills, generous spirit, and bossy loudmouthed personality. She and I got along well, but other girls were a little afraid of her. People often commented on my efficient and organized skills. I enjoyed the fast-paced atmosphere on weekends where the small dining area filled with clanging noises and conversations about the old country. Sometimes a customer came in drunk and bothered us waitresses by disturbing other customers. We tried to get them to leave and even pushed some out the door. If the drunkard didn't leave, my boss made it happen. Her two daughters worked with their mom as well. Their athletic abilities and hard work inspired me to try my best in everything.

If my parents worried about me leaving for Finland, they didn't show it. Since they trusted my friend, Sofia, who was ten years older and from the same church, I'm sure they felt their daughter was in good company. They also didn't have to pay for my trip, as I'd earned my own way. Sofia planned to attend a school in southern Finland, but I kept my plans secret, even from my parents. A tall, slender, single woman, Sofia often wore a smirky smile and tilted her head sideways when she spoke. A little bit of a chatterbox but with her pleasant voice she drew me into all kinds of conversations.

She often would give unsolicited advice if she didn't agree. Though I had not made up my mind, I kept the plan to myself about attending Santala with her in the fall after I'd spent the summer with my relatives in Finland.

Santala, the unique college Sofia had registered to attend, was located in a town called Hanko on the shores of the Gulf of Finland. A multifaceted facility with a denominational seminary, it boasted various educational programs to complete secondary school and vocational training.

Ideally, I would complete school at Santala with Sofia, and my Finnish language skills would improve enough to help me blend into Finland so I wouldn't feel like a foreigner. If I communicated with proper Finnish, I would also learn to write better. My Finnish had become mixed with *Finglish*, part Finn and part English, from living in the cultural hub of Thunder Bay, where many Finnish immigrants hadn't learned English but mixed some words into the Finnish language. For example, people in Finland couldn't understand words like 'kaara' (car) because the word was *auto* in Finnish.

I turned around in the back seat of Dad's Chevy as we drove away from the house to take one last look. About thirty minutes later, Dad parked the vehicle in the small lot at the Thunder Bay International Airport. After we had checked our bags and received our boarding passes, our little group of well-wishers gathered for the last photo before our trip. A single red rose was pinned on our lapels as a parting gift. Since I didn't remember much of my first plane ride from my childhood, the opportunity to travel alone excited me. The flight would take over ten hours with a refueling in Iceland.

I could hardly tame my excitement as we boarded the propeller plane chartered by *Suomi Seura*, a non-profit organization for friends of Finland. It flew only in the summers between Finland and Canada.

The heavy plane rolled slowly on the runway and seemed like it would never lift off. But then it picked up speed and suddenly we were in the air. We left behind small puffs of cloud spread over Lake Superior as the sun peaked on the horizon. With the roar of the engines, conversation became difficult, but soon the plane climbed to its required altitude high above the clouds. I listened as the propellers whizzed then unbuckled my seatbelt to get comfortable. Sofia did the same, and we settled in our seats, waiting for the hot dinner to arrive. She turned to me with her signature wink, and we laughed as we stared out the window. "Look. I love this," I said.

"See those clouds. Isn't God's world amazing?" She sat back in her seat.

I turned away from the window and pulled out a booklet from the pocket in front of me and flipped through the pages. After looking through the beautiful photos of Finland, I made a declaration. "I'm not going back home. I'm going to Santala to finish high school."

"What? That's a surprise. Are you sure? Don't you think you should finish your school back home first? Your Finnish isn't even that good." Sofia had lived in Canada for only three years as an immigrant, but as a mother would in this situation, she expressed concern.

"Yes, I'm sure." After all, I had freedom now to do as I pleased, and Sofia had her own plans. I lacked knowledge and life experience as a cocky teenager. "I'm sure it will all work out when I get there."

"You should have told your parents." Sofia acted as one of our youth leaders at church, so she knew me well enough and wasn't afraid to speak directly.

I tossed my head from side to side and thrust my chin out. "No, I didn't tell them. Why should I? I'm an adult. They'll be okay. I'll let them know later."

"You're only seventeen. That's not an adult!"

I moved my hair out of my eyes. "I'll learn more Finnish. Living with other students on campus sounds like fun. I'll make a lot of friends."

The engines of the flight blasted above the clouds as the flight attendant pushed a cart in the aisle. The fun part about airline travel was the hot meals. Soon I lifted the lid off the plastic container and inhaled the hot aroma of meat and potatoes. "I'm starving."

Sofia continued. "Since I didn't attend a Canadian school and can't advise you on that, did you check on what courses you need to graduate in Finland? I'm sure it's difficult to get a high school diploma within the different systems."

"I'll worry about that later."

The small propeller plane landed in Iceland for fuel, then our journey continued. We remained cramped in place for what seemed like a very long time. After hours and intermittent sleep, the flight landed at Helsinki International Airport and passengers scrambled to collect their belongings. People shoved and pushed as they pulled their carry-ons from the overhead compartment.

Soon we raced to the baggage area and pulled our suitcases from the carousel before departing the airport.

"Hey. My uncle is over there. I have to go." I carried my bag and balanced my purse over my shoulder, legs a little wobbly, and stepped toward my relatives. My uncle and aunt smiled as I approached. I recognized them, even after the eight years since my family immigrated to Canada. All grown into a teenager, they probably didn't recognize me with my business attire of a skirted green two-piece suit. We shook hands.

"Welcome to Finland," my uncle said and picked up my suitcase.

I turned around to Sofia. "Bye for now. See you in Santala," I said. Before Sofia picked up her suitcases, she walked over and gave me a big hug. Then she was gone. I was on my own! The charter company had prearranged our itinerary, and the return flight was in the middle of August and couldn't be changed. *No harm if I don't actually get on the return flight.*

As my uncle drove onto the freeway, my aunt asked, "What are your plans for the summer? Two months is a long time to be away from home."

"I'm not totally sure, but I want to stay at Grandma's for much of the time. This city looks too scary and big."

Helsinki was the capital city of Finland and a cultural and commercial mega with a population of over 600,000 and 1.2 million in the metro area. Though not rich, my relatives lived and worked in the big city. After we drove away from the airport, I noticed the smaller cars and once we arrived in their neighborhood, the crowded sidewalks. The road signs seemed different, but of course, they were in Finnish. Because my life in Canada had been among many Finnish people, the cultural difference wasn't noticeable until later. People in Finland seemed more reserved and talked only when spoken to. That made me, a talkative teenager, uncomfortable at first, but once my relatives got to know me, we got along fine.

The next morning my uncle drove to the bus station where I boarded a luxury bus to *Karstula,* a small town in Central

Finland, to visit my relatives on my mother's side. I sank into the large cushioned seat and surveyed the tall pine trees lined up along the roadside with little underbrush. Who cleaned the long stretches of roadside that looked as if they had been manicured like a city lawn? The government.

After four hours, I arrived at *Kieräperä*, the name of my mother's home. The next morning, I awoke to clanging noises in the kitchen area where utensils clicked against porcelain. Did I miss something? I wasn't sure. At Grandma's, family and visitors alike often gathered around a large table, carrying on like it could be their last meal, conversing, laughing, eating, even shouting. Neighbors who'd become close friends, like family, would drop by any time of day, and my uncle and aunt would invite them in to enjoy whatever cooking was going on.

Like many Finnish households, food was an important part of their culture. On bread baking day, the aroma of rye filled the large kitchen, a deep earthy scent, yet sweet. The Finnish sourdough rye bread, *ruisleipa*, was dark and dense with a heavy crust. No air holes. When cut properly, the rounded shape made firm thin slices which were used for open-faced sandwiches known as *voileipas*. Sometimes my grandma formed the dough into thin doughnut-like shapes which then hung on the pole above the brick oven. Apparently, the older the bread the better, old folks would say. However, the crispy piece could break any chompers if you weren't careful.

Sometimes, immediately after a round loaf slid out of the *leivinuuni*, a sort of wood-fired pizza oven, we would devour it before the crust hardened. We would cut into it to spread butter on the hot mangled slice and enjoy the smooth drip of melted golden liquid that flowed down our chins.

The main living area would have seemed extremely large to me as a child. A daybed filled one corner of the room, while an old rocking chair took a prominent position in the middle. Wooden chairs, placed near the door, provided seating for people to socialize while my aunt made coffee and prepared something to eat if it wasn't during mealtimes. She usually served open-faced sandwiches on sour dark rye bread with real butter and a tomato or cucumber on top. I often wondered why the daybed was in the main living area but later learned that it created a space for the men to lie down for either a nap during the day, after a hard day of physical work, or for the occasional overnight guest.

Back home in Canada, my family had adopted a cross-cultural breakfast of sour rye bread or cinnamon buns with coffee, added to eggs and toast occasionally. Maybe if we were lucky, we would have pancakes with strawberry jam when Mother had the time, or we kids would cook our own. We were immigrants to Canada but often carried old country traditions. Mom or Dad fried eggs in butter, creating a distinct smell in the house, never poached, which I have not gained a taste for even to this day. I usually ate a piece of toast or a store-bought muffin with black coffee. Carrot or oatmeal was my favorite.

Now I had traveled to my grandmother's farm, where an uncle and aunt lived with their four children, my cousins. This was my first visit after our family had immigrated to Canada. The farm was about ten miles from the nearest town, *Karstula*. Since my uncle didn't drive a car, he would often take us kids to town on the back of his tractor.

How I'd missed my favorite childhood farm with all the happy memories of playing with my cousins. The large two-story house was just like I remembered it as a nine-year-old. Small concrete front steps led to a large wooden door. No vibrant colors on either the exterior or interior. Just simple gray or beige. Wheat fields surrounded the house. A barn filled with dozens of cows, calves, and even a horse was situated a little away from the house, on a downward slope. That's where I would find my aunt and uncle in the early morning hours if I wanted to see them milking the cows.

During my visit, I slept on a couch in the front room, a room hardly ever used except on special occasions, like a formal living room. Luckily, I slept through the night even when the sun hardly set in Finland during the summer.

The first morning after arrival, noises coming from the kitchen area awakened me. The rich smells seeping underneath the door made me wonder if it were dinner time. Had I slept that long? *What time is it?*

They used the kitchen area for all occasions when family and visitors gathered together for meals or just to chat and spread gossip around the neighborhood. The aroma of beef roasting in the wood oven reached my nostrils. My ears perked to low voices and people talking among themselves. They probably tried to be quiet since I hadn't joined them yet.

I battled fatigue as I moved in slow motion to push the flowered blanket over to one side. I pulled myself to an upright position at the edge of the bed and rubbed my eyes with the back of my hand until they stung. Somewhere beyond my comprehension, pots and pans clanged so loudly that I turned toward the sound. Someone's feet shuffled on the rough floorboards, probably with slippers made of rough felt and rubber that sounded like a cat scratching a carpet.

At first, I couldn't quite place my whereabouts as the sunlight peeked through the sheer curtains on the large picture window. I groped for the travel bag beside the chair next to my bed. Where was my watch? What time was it? My palms sweat as I read nine o'clock. I didn't know if it was morning or evening since I'd missed a day. As someone who loved her sleep, I could easily nap through the day and not blink an eye about it, jetlagged or not.

My hardcover blue suitcase stood in the corner of the large room. As soon as I dressed in day clothes, a soft knock came. My aunt said, "It's breakfast time." I quickly acclimatized to the situation. My aunt spoke in a soft voice, careful not to enter the room. A strong flavor of pot roast accosted me and hazy smoke filled the open doorway, probably from frying butter on the old cast-iron frying pan that was used to make gravy on the wood-burning stove.

I clasped my hands above my head. "It's already nine in the morning. I slept in. Sorry." At Grandma's house, the family gathered around the humongous wooden table in the great room, also known as the kitchen, that served as an everything-happens-here piece of furniture. I wondered how long people could sit on those wooden benches without backrests. The wood cookstove with a massive brick oven served as the central piece of décor in the large kitchen.

I strolled into the kitchen. "It's not dinner yet!" I don't do mornings well, but I smiled sheepishly and looked around for a space to sit.

"Come and have some roast, boiled potatoes, and gravy," my uncle mumbled, chewing on a piece of homemade sour rye bread as he pointed to the end of the bench. "We've been up since six o'clock milking cows. They need to be fed and milked before anyone else gets any food."

"I can't eat meat and potatoes for breakfast. Do you have any strong Finnish coffee with a cinnamon bun? I still crave them from when I used to stay here as a kid."

My favorite uncle, the loudest and funniest of all of them, laughed and wiggled his eyebrows and turned to his wife. "Go get the girl her *pulla*!"

I took a whiff of the coffee and splashed in some milk from the pitcher, then took a sip. *What is this?* Too much milk. Too little coffee. Then I realized it was cow's milk—from this morning's milking! It didn't smell bad nor look any different from store-bought milk, but its thick creamy taste I would need to get used to while here.

I still had a decision to make about living in Finland. Would I attend school here or not?

2

a foreign address

FULL OF FEAR and anxiety, I chose to come back home to finish my education and find God's plan. Two years after my trip to Finland, life slipped into the typical routine of teenage girls: socialize, talk on the phone, attend school, hang out, and work. For me, attending church remained important, but change loomed on the horizon.

When the service ended, as per our custom, many of us young people hung out together in someone's home. We all lived in a cultural bubble with other immigrant families and conversed in Finnish, our native language. As young people, we preferred to speak to each other in English. The girls in the church became close friends. I also wrote to girls in Finland.

Our small group was comprised mostly of females and a few younger guys of all different ages. They had given me the nickname Parrot, as I repeated words and talked too much, a chatterbox maybe. Since I was younger than others, my peers teased me a lot. Even some adults called me by the nickname. Others seemed to enjoy making fun of me even though I didn't always like it, and I frowned sometimes when it became too much. I learned to live with it.

Would I ever get married or would I remain a spinster? Sure. One day. *I plan a life of travel and then I'll settle down with a certain someone.* A quote from my high school yearbook. Silly, I had no prospects, and any dates usually ended before the second one. Or the guys were jerks, unbelievers, or just plain boring. They, meaning invisible church rules, had warned me about going out with unbelievers. Therefore, I ended any such dates as quickly as they started. One self-absorbed guy who smelled like a smokestack made it easy to keep my distance— until he tried to cross the line. That was the end of him! Another one tricked me into coming inside his bachelor pad. My stupidity! Fortunately, his shyness created distance, but I bolted out and never saw him again.

I lived at home with my mother and father and my six siblings, three brothers and three sisters, me being the oldest. As an immigrant family, we kids learned to fend for ourselves and wore second-hand clothing. Bags of groceries appeared at our doorstep often. We had lived in several places before my parents purchased the small house on Winnipeg Avenue when I was ten or eleven. It was situated on the poor part of the long street, while prestigious large houses lined the other end. The house proved inadequate for our large family. So, somehow, my parents received a loan to renovate by adding a basement and three rooms on the main level.

I was overjoyed when my sister Hilla and I got our own room at the front of the house beside the living room. Both parents enjoyed company, my father more than my mother, so they allowed us kids to have friends over. In fact, many friends liked to come over, and my best girlfriend, Lahja, slept at our house often. The age difference between us siblings of one or two years meant we shared a lot of the same friends, though each of us had our individual close ones. Noise and play filled our home. I disdained chaos and tried to keep order. When I came home, I often said to my siblings, "What's going on here?"

The noise didn't seem to bother our father, as he could easily saw logs (snore) on the couch after a hard day's work cutting trees. Was he deaf?

A rotary phone was attached to the wall near a bedroom. The long cord came in handy when anyone needed privacy and quiet, so we pulled the cord into the bedroom and closed the door as much as possible, hoping that no one would press the lever to cut the conversation. It became a problem when more than one person wanted to use the phone. Patience wasn't a virtue of mine. I would try to get someone's attention with a quick click on the lever to show I needed the phone. I personally might have taken advantage of my position as the firstborn to get my way too many times.

One day, I pulled the receiver with the long cord into the bedroom and chatted with a girlfriend about my future plans. At nineteen, we had talked about boyfriends and what kind of qualities each of us looked for in a future husband. I don't remember what she shared, but I know one important aspect I wanted in a husband. He would have to be a Christian. Of course, I had a few other requests. I also listed what I didn't like in a guy, but God has a sense of humor. Would He listen to my ramblings and grant my requests, especially as a teen girl who seemed clueless as to what would be best for her in a life partner?

On a Saturday evening in June, I walked with Sofia on our way to church for a prayer meeting, an event I enjoyed and attended often. Suddenly, she said, "I've been thinking for two weeks about this guy back in Finland."

Before she could continue, I laughed and interrupted. "Did you meet someone over there?" Excitement filled me as I glanced at her and continued, without letting her finish her thoughts. "That's so great." Since she had attended Bible college in Finland, it wouldn't surprise me if she found someone. After all, she neared thirty. She laughed with me, not at me, and didn't even get upset when I blurted out, "Do you think you'll go back to Finland someday?" I had a habit of speaking before thinking.

Almost at the church, she continued, "No. I met a young seminary student, but that's not it." She smirked.

I paused and turned to face her and placed my hands on my hips. "Then what is it? Say it."

She flashed a mischievous grin. "He wrote and asked me if I knew anyone in Canada who could write to him as a pen pal to teach him English."

As a teenager, I divided my time between school, work, and activities with the church youth group. I also taught Sunday school. Was she insinuating I should? Did I need another responsibility to add to my already busy agenda? If I agreed, I would keep it as a duty. Loyalty was one of my character traits.

Although she hadn't asked me directly, I answered, "I don't know. Can't you get some guy to write him?"

"We don't have anyone else in the church who can write in Finnish and English. Markus is the only one, but though he speaks Finnish, he can't write it. And I certainly cannot write in English," Sofia said.

She reached into her purse and pulled out a black and white grainy photo of a group of students from the school she had attended—Santala, the one I planned to attend but didn't. I studied the photo, trying to make out a small face. The guy had glasses and light brown hair that receded a bit. After a few minutes, I answered, "Okay, I guess there's no harm in writing. He's across the ocean, anyway. I'll never see him."

"Think about it," Sofia said.

We arrived at the church when I realized something strange. *Why now?* Would he receive my letter in time for me to receive a reply, even if he answered right away? Back in January, I had booked a charter flight to Finland that left the following week to visit my relatives with my sister and Mom. Maybe I'd write after I returned home or while in Finland.

At home, I told my mom, and she said little, so I left it at that. A few days later, I wrote and told him about my visit to Finland. *Wouldn't it be interesting if we met?*

Thunder Bay
June 8, 1970

Hello Antti,

I rejoiced when Sofia asked me to write because I've always wanted another pen pal. It's fun to receive letters from Finland, especially from Christians. I write to my girlfriend over there, but she's not a Christian. There's so much to write when both have found Jesus as Savior.

I've lived in Canada for ten years. We have seven children in our family and I am the oldest. Since I grew up in a Christian family, I was saved when I was eleven years old at a Pentecostal Bible camp. It was there I realized I was a sinner and needed Christ in my life. From that day on, my life changed, but I was too shy to tell anybody about my experience. As

26

a result, I backslid and again at fourteen met Christ and was baptized. I thank my Lord that He cares for me and keeps me. We have a wonderful Savior who hears our prayers.

Right now, I have great cause to be thankful because it was through a miracle that I received the opportunity to visit Finland this summer. As a student, I do not have the money for such a long trip, but my God is rich. Both my mother and younger sister are also visiting Finland this summer. If God wills, I will be in Finland on June 21. If you have time and want, you can write to my uncle's address near Helsinki (uncle's address supplied).

I'm from Central Finland, Karstula, so I'm sure I will spend the most time there. My Finland trip lasts until the end of August. I'm also going to Lahti for the conference.

Sofia told me that you're traveling with the tent all summer. I'm sure your time will be spent. May the Lord bless your work as you witness about Jesus. I've told you a little about myself, but it would be nice to hear about you. Write in English.

Jesus with you,
Pirkko Paananen (home address supplied)

I folded the letter into an airmail envelope and dropped it into the mailbox and forgot about it until I arrived in Finland at my aunt's house.

3

the encounter

WE ARRIVED AT my uncle's home in Finland, and after
our greetings, his wife handed me an envelope with a funny
smile. "This came for you. Who's it from? Mysterious."

I thought for a moment. "It's from a guy I wrote to. He's
my new pen pal."

Why didn't he include a return address? Later that evening
in the bedroom, I found the answer in the letter. Antti had
disclosed several addresses and a detailed itinerary for the next
few months until school started at the end of August. His
summer job entailed travel all over Finland.

Kiponiemi, Finland
June 17, 1970

Peace in Christ Pirkko,

Thank you for your letter that surprised me. I received it when I arrived home from meetings in Turku. Greetings from Kiponniemi, the Finnish Free Church camp. I am here this midsummer week as a youth leader and general worker. I just led our campfire session where we felt how God blessed us. It's wonderful to be a young Christian experiencing the heavenly joy of salvation in the heart, with sins forgiven. Jesus has taken care of them by His shed blood at Calvary. Amazing to be in His work, in the fields, now when the time is still here, and see people's hunger to experience something from what Jesus can give. Last week, we witnessed many souls give their lives to Jesus. Thank you, Lord!

I am traveling with the Free Church large crusade tent which seats about 1500-2000 people. It travels to many cities.

Sofia already told you I'm attending seminary with the Free Church denomination. Since I already said what I was doing, I will introduce myself. I'm from Central Finland, Sumiainen, Viitakyla, where I lived until age sixteen when my family moved to Lahti, where we have lived for eight years. I am twenty-four years old. There are five children. I'm the second oldest of three boys and two girls. I received salvation as a thirteen-year-old boy at a Christian club, and from then on, I've walked the life of faith, although fumbling in the beginning. Thank God that His Son, Jesus, keeps us on the path. I received the call into ministry as a teenager when I got saved. But I've only been in full-time ministry for a little over two years. The seminary still lasts three more years. I've completed one year already. That is it about me for now. More later.

It surprised me when I got your letter. I wrote to Sofia and told her I don't understand enough to reply in English. I understood your writing with help from a dictionary. Just write the same way, but not any more difficult. I am happy if you write. When you write, include some English and some Finnish.

You must be excited to visit Finland. We'll meet at the conference. I don't know you. How can we connect and find each other?
Blessed greetings,
Antti

How did he describe himself? He didn't. Only that he was twenty-four years old. That seemed so old! Without a physical description, I did not know what he looked like beyond the tiny image in the photograph Sofia shared. He worked in ministry and interned as the summer tent crusade manager for the Free Church of Finland denomination, traveling all over the country planning meetings and serving well-known preachers. He laid out his full itinerary in his first letter! I did not need a summary of his work, though it would be nice to meet, at least once.

We both grew up in Christian families and were saved as children. And both families belonged to the same denomination, in different countries. Was this a God connection or just an interesting comparison? He had finished the one-year youth leadership program and one year of seminary and had three more to graduation.

According to plan, my mom, sister, and I were at the summer conference in Lahti when something strange happened.

We were inside the tent before the meeting began. I'm often late for places, but this time I arrived early in case I recognized Antti, as if doing surveillance. The grainy black-and-white group photo Sofia showed me helped me visualize what he might look like in real life. If I saw him first, I could pretend I didn't show up if I didn't like the looks of him. Not really. If we were to continue writing as pen pals, it made no difference with 6,000 miles of ocean between us. I had no inkling of anything more than a teacher/student relationship. Assisting others came easy to me, and, as the firstborn, I translated for my parents since they didn't speak English. Perhaps a friendship? I meandered through the crowd and kept an eye out for a guy with glasses and light brown hair. Was he short or tall? Fat or skinny? How would he dress? How are you supposed to meet someone among thousands of people?

Antti worked throughout the grounds organizing things. He prepared the sound system and platform for the preachers and singers as well as welcomed people. At one point, I think I recognized him when he rushed by, and he possibly even shook my hand as an unofficial greeter. Or was that him? I watched as he chatted with friends or family who gathered from all over Finland. This guy sure looked like him, but I thought little of it, as the meeting was about to begin and we needed to locate our seats in the large tent. I couldn't believe I had never described my physical appearance. Neither had he.

My heart filled with joy as the singers erupted into hymns that I recognized. The sermons also blessed me along with the fact that I was among so many Christian young people gathered in one place, something I had not experienced back home. After the meeting ended, we had already moved to the back when I heard these words, "If Pirkko Paananen is in the tent, please come to the front of the platform." The strange voice boomed from the speakers.

Someone asked for me? Then I remembered. I turned toward the front as my hand flew to my chest and realized it must be him. After all, we had agreed upon a meeting at this conference. I'm sure my face morphed into all shades of red or purple. The heat in my neck traveled to my chin as I contemplated my next move.

Many people had already left the tent. Only a few would see me march up the aisle or hear my feet crush the ground while my heart pounded in my chest. Did I look acceptable? My hair, in a beehive bun, was at least a proper Christian style, but something else bothered me. What if my dress was too short for such a holy place as the altar? I'd just arrived in Finland so my "American style" might not blend in with the modern styles of the youth here. Finland had always been progressive in fashion, which the young adhered to. Finnish people lumped Canadians and Americans into one category. I wore a knitted blue dress with short sleeves and a rounded collar, perhaps a little outdated.

I watched the man I surveyed early on as he hopped off the platform and extended his hand for a handshake. "Hello. I'm Antti."

I joked around. "Hi, how do you do it? Such a small man and such a big tent?" I laughed longer than normal and bit my lip. I stepped back. His facial expression provided no clue as to what he thought. My perceived freedom to express myself didn't always come out right. My friends had told me I talked too much out of turn and often put my foot in my mouth. A blooper I wish I could take back.

After an awkward moment, he replied with confidence, "Nice to meet in person." He ignored my comment about the tent. I knew we characterized Finnish people as reserved and serious and private, especially with strangers. Their conversations lacked small talk. If you asked, "How are you?" people would probably give an account of their day. It wouldn't be considered a casual question. So, I wondered about this man. Was he a conversationalist? Not at all a joker, judging by first impressions. Or the silent analytical type?

Antti wore a diagonally striped brown and black tie that matched his brown pants. His white shirt, with sleeves rolled above the elbow, showed he was working. Tinted glasses covered his eyes so I couldn't tell what color they were, not that I would dare to look him in the eye. He had light brown hair cut short with a part at the side. A questioning look in his eyes seemed to say, "Who is this girl?" I sized him up as a serious, no-nonsense guy with a pleasant face. Nothing sparked, no romanticizing. Only surprised by his short stature, I had no other thoughts about this friendly young student. Just another Finnish young man, like many I'd met back home in Thunder Bay.

"Yes. I'm sorry. I should at least introduce you to my mom and sister Hilla." They both turned and gave a quick handshake. "I see you have a camera like I do. I love taking photos everywhere I go. Here's a good place to steal one of you, just so I don't forget."

We had already stepped outside the tent and snapped photos of each other. He excused himself to set up the sound for the next meeting that would soon start. A quick meet and greet, but we made plans for him to drive me around his hometown of Lahti the very next day.

Though I accepted the free sightseeing tour, I'd experienced no kind of flutter other than as a person to teach English to. I would answer his questions, divulging a little about myself.

Lahti was a city about the same size as Thunder Bay in southern Finland, about an hour's drive from Helsinki.

Antti arrived at my aunt's house on Monday afternoon in his brother's Volvo. I should have been nervous, but somehow, I trusted this man, even though we were strangers and alone.

I started the conversation. "How big is Lahti?"

"About 120,000. Do you want to see the ski hills?"

He drove out of town to the famous *Salpausselkä*, a sports center featuring ski jumps and trails that held national competitions during winter.

He stopped the car in the empty parking space, and we remained in the vehicle. "It's amazing. I'm impressed. I like cross-country skiing but would never try ski jumping. It looks so scary."

"I cross-country ski a lot too." Then he explained how this place was a famous tourist attraction. Later, as we drove through downtown and other areas, I sensed his pride regarding his hometown.

As a busy man, Antti dropped me off after an hour, as he needed to get back to dismantle the crusade tent.

We met once more at a coffee shop a few weeks later in *Jyväskylä,* where he worked at another tent crusade. The city was on the way to my relatives in Central Finland, which made it convenient for a quick stopover.

I don't remember what we talked about except that he shared his desire to come to Canada to study English. I sensed his passion for ministry, which I could not reciprocate, and his serious interest in learning English.

He shared about his life's goal of becoming a missionary in Ecuador and his calling to missions as a young boy. "I know that there will be many trials before I can step into God's plan. It's going to be hard." I could sense his excitement about the ministry, especially when he explained what he learned from seasoned missionaries.

I sipped my coffee, alternating with a bite from a sweet roll in my other hand. "I'm not sure about a career. I still have a year of high school before I can apply to university."

Antti's eyes lowered to his empty cup. I noticed he hesitated about something. Then he offered me spiritual advice. "Seek God about what He wants you to do."

I'm sure he thought I was so immature and confused. Was he interested in me? I didn't notice, and I certainly wasn't interested. I had a flight to catch back home to Canada!

4

prophetic words

MY MEANDERING EDUCATIONAL path began in grade nine with no guidance from my parents. After all, they could not even speak rudimentary English, so I needed to trust the guidance of counselors and teachers. They directed me to the commercial program that led to a secretarial/bookkeeping vocation. In those days, there were three programs in high school: commercial, technical, and academic.

This decision created obstacles to entering university when I later realized it was the wrong choice. I graduated with a commercial diploma and faced a dilemma. I wanted to attend university, but what would I study? In Ontario, I needed the academic diploma, so I entered my fifth year, grade 13, of high school while studying Spanish at our local university to fulfill credit requirements. Fortunately, with hard work, I excelled and succeeded even though I lacked some academic prerequisites. I believed in myself even though I battled poor self-esteem, eventually developing a determined attitude.

In the fall of 1970, I received a letter from Antti explaining he wasn't able to come to Canada the next summer. No Visa. But he talked about studying English regardless, perhaps in England. His missionary mentors informed him that they needed seminary graduates in Ecuador to train local pastors, and he did not intend to let his plans go astray. I admired his certainty in his life's goal, as well as his tenacity to learn English.

During the Christmas holidays, I wrote about school, family, and church. Then I wrote a story about the birth of Jesus and sent it to him, as if he didn't know the scriptural account. To prove I was smart, I explained my educational path. The year before, I completed eight subjects and didn't have to write the final exams in June. We had exams just before Christmas and again before Easter, and then once more in June. But if your marks averaged over a certain percentage, you were exempt from the finals. I did it. No exams in June, so now I studied hard to avoid the finals this June.

Seeking God's direction obsessed me so much that I wrote about it all the time. My lack of direction and all the plans I'd created in my head scared me. But I was thankful for a friend to share my worries, even by letter. As our correspondence progressed to a soulmate status, I divulged more about my life. He was a guy, and we were at odds on many issues and I feared what he would think of me. Regardless of our shared vision to do God's work, we didn't agree on which country. He felt called to Ecuador, while I wanted to stay in Canada.

At home, I lived a life of extreme dedication to our church. Even as a child, I loved prayer meetings. My pen pal became my emotional landing place for sharing struggles I experienced with our church. My mother and father, along with a few other people, pioneered our Finnish language local church in the early 1960s. Before the new church had a regular pastor, guest speakers would come to preach. People came to hear the gospel, and many immigrants believed in Jesus as their personal Savior. This group gathered as a little congregation called the Finnish Free Church, a denomination my parents were a part of in Finland.

One speaker, Pastor Mayblom from Maine, inspired me to seek after the Holy Spirit, which I yearned to understand better. As a teenager, the discord between the local Finnish Saalem Pentecostal Church and our church, the Finnish Free Church, saddened me as well as the young people in both churches. Often, our youth groups joined for gatherings. Weren't we all Christians who should rejoice when souls get saved and added to the family of God?

I'm not sure why, but another guest speaker who came from Finland, Juho Koivumaki, a well-known evangelist, spoke over me, "I will come back for your wedding." Marriage was not on my mind nor was I even dating anyone so I hid this in my heart.

I replied, "Then you won't ever come back, or if you do, it won't be for a very long time!"

I yearned to write to Antti about my dream of becoming a teacher but put it off for fear of rejection. It made little sense since we had not even dated, and his opinions shouldn't matter. But underneath the outer layer of my carefree spirit, I became attached spiritually and emotionally. He wrote about his traditional views about the wife of a missionary, something I wasn't interested in. Many of his friends prepared for pastoral ministry or the mission field. A nursing career would be best for a missionary wife, so I thought.

I never considered becoming a pastor's wife. In my mind, I could not fit into that kind of role. The examples I'd seen growing up in the church didn't appeal. One wife had been caring, kind, humble, and a prayer warrior. Others worked in careers of their own and supplemented the family income. They all served their husbands and the church and projected a cheerful attitude, regardless of fears or pain they may have carried. Besides, I didn't play the piano! And worst of all, they were all poor, having to depend on handouts at times, much like my family. And the pastors in our small church also worked in manual labor for extra income. As an immature teenager, I needed some attitude adjusting.

A career in education interested me for about a year before I expressed the idea to Antti. At first, I shared my dream with Lahja, my girlfriend who married and had a baby already. "I plan to go to university and become a teacher."

She responded, "Why? I thought you didn't like school?"

"Well, I've changed my mind. I want to help young people." It was time to let go of the immature babble that kept me in so much indecisiveness. Actually, my grade 13 geography teacher, Miss Dennis, inspired me to realize that I liked geography and how it would fit my goal of travel. One time, she even left me in charge of the class while she stepped out. I survived the paper airplanes and the constant chatter of my fellow students.

A few days later, I worked up enough courage to inform my pen pal and added a dangerous prayer to God, "Lead me wherever you want me." After Antti's many inquiries, I wrote, "I never planned on teaching as a career, but last fall I began dreaming about it. I didn't know why I wanted to attend university, but now I'm assured. I want to become a teacher."

"Why didn't you tell me earlier about this?" This reply wasn't what I expected. Why did it matter to him anyway? He was studying to be a pastor or missionary, and I would study to become a high school teacher and needed to start university in September 1971. A hint of disappointment seeped through his next few letters, but he added, "Maybe God will allow me to visit there before I go to the mission field." He tried to encourage me. "If you one day feel sure about God's call, the devil will try to make it useless. You will know."

Then, after telling him my future plans to pursue teaching, I also wrote about what I'd sensed for a few years but never shared with anyone. Recognizing God's approval made me realize He was calling me to go. Where? I needed to find out.

One thing led to another, and I attended the Finnish Pentecostal annual summer conference. The meetings were emotionally charged, and the presence of the Holy Spirit touched many lives. At one point, I sensed God spoke to me in a meeting where they presented missions to Canada. The words of a Finnish song burned in my spirit, loosely translated, "The Lord lovingly calls, who would hurry into the fields, souls lost in sin, tell them about Jesus' grace, speak Lord, with a joyful answer, 'Send me'." I remembered a congregant of my church years earlier who spoke a prophetic word that God wanted to use me, even with my low sense of self-worth. I dismissed it. Through these spiritual experiences, I sensed God's direction for my life, especially since Antti's correspondence encouraged me to seek God's plan with abandonment.

5

different sides of family

I DIDN'T REPLY to Antti's every letter and postcard in a timely fashion for several reasons. First, I didn't want him to think I was too anxious or to give him the wrong idea. Second, my life seemed too complicated with work, school, church, family, and friends. Third, I was ashamed to share about the family issues, especially with my younger sister.

In early February, my father returned from a preaching trip to Finland after six weeks away from home. I rejoiced to see him back in the house. My sister Laura caused worry for Mom and me, and we squabbled about her behavior. Even Mom couldn't always control her and didn't know where she took off to. My father's authoritarian style of parenting conflicted with our mother's free spirit. My parents perceived me as a church-going good girl, and they didn't question me about anything.

Dad tried to discipline us kids and it often turned into shouting matches. He lacked instructional skills but displayed his unpredictable temper by yelling at us for no reason. We would argue when he commanded orders or we stormed into our rooms. Once the shouting ended, he acted as if nothing happened and plopped himself on the couch like a big old cuddly bear. Dad's different sides mystified us. Happy and engaging one moment and the grizzly the next. His negative words reinforced our mistakes and damaged our self-esteem, and he withheld affirmation when we should have received it.

Mom remained the calming influence in our home and knew how to handle her husband when needed, but her phlegmatic personality didn't help during a conflict. She had to care for a houseful of kids alone, as our father worked out of town during the week.

WHEN I WAS thirteen and fourteen, we lived in Nakina, a small mill town north of Thunder Bay. One day Dad took some of us kids for a drive on a private bush road in a remote location somewhere in Northern Ontario. How many kids loaded into the 1959 gray Chevy I don't recall. The one with wings for tail lights. As we sped on the bumpy dirt road, the car jerked and my head bumped on the back of the front seat. I screamed, "What's going on?" Was he going to spank us for fighting or what? Or was there a fire somewhere? "Why are we stopping in the middle of nowhere?" I hollered from the back seat.

The abrupt stop was an example of his maneuvers with his heavy foot while driving. One moment his foot was on the accelerator and the next on the brake. Who knows how many brake pads he had changed in his lifetime?

A dust cloud billowed behind us, and when he opened the door, I almost choked from the poison that accosted us. He handed me the keys and said, "You're going to drive." I was shocked since I'd never sat in the driver's seat. My eyes widened, but at thirteen and small for my age, when I climbed into the seat, I found I couldn't reach the pedals. I wiggled to the edge of the seat. He seemed determined to teach his daughter to drive. He pointed to the gearshift. My hand trembled when I touched it. Somehow, I pushed the accelerator, and the car jerked forward and almost ran him over while he was walking to the passenger side.

With his gruff voice, he said, "Drive." No instructions followed. How was I supposed to know how to drive without a teacher? His motto: I should know how to do it by watching him. After I shifted into gear, the car jerked forward, even worse than the first time. I held onto the steering wheel while my knuckles turned white. I maintained a tight grip. The car veered toward the left. Soon we were on the other side of the road. Dad yelled, "Turn the wheel!"

"Which way?" I yelled back in a panic. Soon the car slid toward a sloping ditch. Dry brushes and twigs cracked as the machine jerked past tall grassy shrubs.

Then it happened!

He plunked his heavy work boot on my size five foot. I screamed as the Chevy stopped with its long nose halfway into the ditch. What was that? I pulled my throbbing foot onto the seat as Dad shoved the gear into park.

My driving lesson with Dad didn't end there. After a few more close calls with curbs and a couple of road tests, I received my driver's license. Dad's methods may have been unorthodox but his heart was in the right place. He showed his love by trusting me with his prize possession, his Chevy.

We moved back to Port Arthur, where I started my first part-time job as a waitress at age fifteen. I was elated with the money but not so much with the job at a dingy restaurant. It provided me with the opportunity to buy my own clothes. Otherwise, I would've had hand-me-downs like the rest of my siblings. I enjoyed dressing well but did not wear makeup because of some unwritten rule that our church followed.

When Dad was away, I ran errands for everybody since I borrowed his car. But the biggest energy drain involved driving around the streets of our city at all hours of the night looking for Laura. Asking for prayer for her filled many of my letters, as well as complaints that God hadn't answered our prayers. Preachers warned us about backsliding and to be on the lookout for the enemy who prowls about like a roaring lion. Some turned away from faith but returned to God after a personal spiritual experience. At fourteen, Laura had not yet fallen away from the love of God but played close to the edge of the enemy's camp too often. When would things turn around?

When I stressed over unanswered prayers, Antti's letters encouraged me. Often, I sensed he waited in suspense, wanting to hear how God guided me. He seemed eager to know as much as I did, maybe even more. As of February, my last year in high school, I wondered about my next year and what program would accept me because of my sketchy academic background. However, I kept thinking about university as the right direction.

In late February, Antti wrote, "My life hasn't been easy and when I was twenty, everything was hard with many problems. It wasn't easy to choose life's calling. I had no miraculous vision about missions, but God spoke and gave an inner calling, and that I cannot disobey." This encouraged me to keep on seeking God's direction.

We encouraged each other about spiritual lessons while seeking direction, and I believed God had a purpose for my life. Why did we keep writing about God's plan and for me to understand God's guidance? Was there an inner knowing on his part as he wrote the following emphatic words? "What you feel in your heart may be God's calling. If it's from Him, he will assure you. If you didn't fear it, then it could be just your own plan you want for yourself." The apostle Paul reminds us that God chooses the foolish to confound the wise. And that is so true. I was unsure of myself and what God wanted me to do in life. By this time, I had forgotten about my desire for a Christian husband or my surrender to God many moons earlier.

Antti attended a friend's wedding in Finland, then wrote these words: "Perhaps one day it will be my turn. I've been praying that I won't make a mistake regarding marriage!" *What was he saying?*

While Antti applied to study at a language school in England for the summer, I applied to university in Canada. In April I received an acceptance letter to a college in Toronto but vacillated between two ideas. Go to Israel with Sofia? Go to university for four years? Though I dreamed of travel, it didn't seem practical. And where would I get the money from anyway? At nineteen, I pondered the economy and how many university graduates had jobs. Would the four years of study be a waste when I could use my decent skills for a clerical job already? Debt scared me. Perhaps my hopes and dreams for a normal Christian husband and family would have to wait for a long time, at least until I graduated and achieved a respectable career.

Just before the application date would expire, I applied to Western University in London, Ontario. They had the only suitable program. Because I had studied so many business subjects in high school, the Secretarial Science (Business Administration) program would be a sure fit. And it was...until it wasn't.

My life deviated from my friends' in several ways. We all grew up in the Finnish cultural bubble, where we associated with our own kind, even in high school. Thunder Bay was known as the city with the highest Finnish population outside of Finland. Finns made up our cross-country ski team at school, which I was a part of. Skiing was something we did, even if sports weren't our thing.

My girlfriend, two years older and like a sister to me, kept me grounded. Though we were both short, we argued about who was shorter. I won by about half an inch, but her hair was blonder. Lahja was my north star. I believed her Christian influence kept me on the straight and narrow, though I kept my escapades with unbeliever guys from her. We did so much together, even went to the school's football games, although we understood nothing. She met her tall handsome guy from Toronto, and they insisted on a wedding in the freezing temperatures.

"Why do you have to have the wedding in the middle of January? Can't you wait until the summer? Even spring would be better. And besides, if I'm going to be your maid of honor, I will need a dress that covers my neck."

"Well, my fiancé doesn't want to wait until summer. Why not have it sooner rather than later?" She always had answers for me that made sense, but I wasn't convinced. The problem with my eczema that flared up, especially in the winter, caused me anxiety.

We often had sleepovers at each other's houses so we were aware health issues that we experienced. I often moaned about my problematic skin condition that worsened at inopportune times. Just before her wedding, anxiety raised its ugly head as red blotches appeared on my neck. How would it have looked with a low-cut dress? Aware my eczema often flared up in the winter, she came up with a solution that suited my situation and their winter wedding. She opted for high-collar, white frilly blouses with green velvet long skirts for her bridal party girls.

After Lahja married and many others became mothers, I didn't fit in anymore. Determination led me to find a different path: leave town, explore, travel, study at university, and forge a career. And one day, far into the future, marry my prince charming—tall, dark, and handsome…a professor, well-educated, and a Christian.

I continued seeking God's will for my life as our correspondence turned a corner. We'd veered from an English teacher/student relationship to a counselor/counselee relationship.

Thunder Bay
May 26, 1971

Dear Antti,

…I was glad to hear that your tests, especially English, went so well. This year has been a challenge because it's the year that prepares students for higher education. Often, I think and wonder how I have done as well as I have. But the only conclusion that I can come up with is that God has been working on me.

…Last week I saw His Land, a film about Israel. After the film, I longed to go there. Israel, the clock of our time, is the most beautiful country. I wish I could walk on the streets of Jerusalem and the Mount of Olives.

...I'm realizing that He doesn't tell everyone what He wants. I think I have been waiting for some special sign that would show His plan. God doesn't work that way. We cannot direct Him by asking Him to do a certain thing the way we want it to happen. I think, if I had my own way up to this point, I would not be at home anymore or at school.
   Jesus with you,
   Pirkko

My heart filled with gratitude. My soulmate listened, via letters, to my anxieties and helped carry them to God in prayer. Another reason my spiritual life grew important to me, besides seeking God's direction for my life, was to pray for my sister and her friends. I asked God, "Why them? Why not me?" One day the authorities caught them drinking and my sister had to attend court. The incident devastated my parents, but they filed the secret away in a lockbox of shame. We never talked about it. It could have happened to me or anyone, but I had no interest in alcohol or drugs. Was it because God had a different path aligned for me and, by His grace, He saved me from self-harm?

I prepared myself for the next step. I would leave home and church and find my way in a new city. A step of faith. My childlike faith kept me trusting God for His direction. During a conference in August, a guy offered me a sixteen-hour ride to Toronto, where I would stay overnight at a friend's house. Then, in the morning, I took the train to London to visit the university and hunt for an apartment. Somehow, I made it to the university early enough to peruse through the list of student housing before other students arrived. I didn't want to live on campus, which would have been awkward since I came from a sheltered immigrant background and didn't feel I'd fit in. Besides, I had never partied. Never been to a school dance.

Never been to a movie. Never tasted alcohol, drugs, or cigarettes. I hadn't even attended the prom or my high school graduation. Would I make it through university unscathed?

I wrote to Antti about my experience. "I found the perfect housing with an old senior couple who don't smoke or drink, within walking distance to the university. A single room on the main floor and a shared kitchen and bathroom with them, and the rent is cheap."

On the way to the railroad station, I strolled the streets of London and reflected on God's direction and the new adventure ahead. But one thing would change. I could no longer attend a Finnish church. I would have to search for a Canadian church, which would be so different and large, nothing like my church with forty to fifty people, where everyone, young and old, knew everything about each other.

When I arrived back in Thunder Bay, my job kept me busy, as well involvement at the church. Like many times before I scribbled another six-page letter at my desk, which faced the window overlooking the street, reminiscing about our relationship while my siblings played in the next room.

Our home was a beehive of activity. My younger siblings often brought friends over, and with seven kids, visits happened often. Neighborhood boys and girls enjoyed coming to our house, as we were free to play and make noise or horse around. My parents also enjoyed the company. The kitchen served as a communal kitchen where we older kids made our own meals of mac and cheese whenever Mom was busy with babies or toddlers.

Near the end of summer, just before I left for university. I received a letter that bothered me. I shifted, unable to find a comfortable spot on my bed. I needed alone time in my room and hoped no one would disrupt my concentration. With sweaty fingers, I ripped the envelope. But before I unfolded the flimsy paper, the kind used to reduce the cost of postage based on weight, my thoughts wandered to worst-case scenarios. What if he now stopped writing because I had revealed my plans to him? What if he considered a girlfriend more closely suitable to his mission's goal? What if he didn't agree with my career goal? Assumptions could drive me crazy if I dwelled on them.

When I read his letter, I grew conflicted. Why? Perhaps it was my imagination that he would now seek God for the type of life partner whom he needed to fulfill his dream of being a missionary to Ecuador. He wrote, "I received assurance from God as to whether I will go there alone or with someone else. God can call a partner or a helpmate." *Why did this bother me? We weren't even dating. And why did it sound like I had let him down?*

Later, I noticed how his writing had turned to past tense when he described his feelings about our pen pal relationship. "Remember when we met in Lahti a year ago and you didn't say who you were when I greeted you, and I had to call you on the loudspeaker?" Was that a rebuke? Or did he realize I'd been avoiding him? Was this the end of our letter writing? It's easy to misinterpret words on paper, especially when we'd never spent much time together in person, only twice, an hour or two each time. A conversation would solve all kinds of misunderstandings. But that was not possible.

6

settling in

I MOVED TO London at the beginning of September 1971, though classes didn't start until the twentieth. I loved my new address on a street lined with old two-story brick houses with beautiful mature trees on boulevards. Large maples adorned front yards, as seen in many heritage areas of London. The porch wrapped around the side of the house enclosed by a white spindle railing that was about two feet high. My room faced the street, and I could follow the action from the large window. Shutters on the sides of the window added elegance. Thick fabric curtains ensured privacy. Anyone working on the roof would need secure ladders to stay safe on the high roof which steepled like a church.

The first time I climbed the few steps to the landing, I noticed the black mailbox on the left side of the door, an important feature for me as long as we continued to correspond. Still perplexed, I expected we would continue writing, so I provided Antti with my new address, hoping to hear from him. My mind played all kinds of tricks about this. Would he discontinue writing? His definite goal for the mission field and dream of a partner called by God was at the forefront of my mind. And a missionary wife who fit into the traditional role of nursing… Did he still adhere to this?

Though I didn't live on campus, I was about a ten-minute bus ride away, or a half an hour's walk, which I preferred. I had a walking habit as my high school was about twenty minutes away from home, and I enjoyed the physical exercise which provided time for meditation. Would anyone ask me for a date here at the university? Anything would be an improvement after my five years of high school with a nearly non-existent dating life. By October, I had one date. I didn't even know what a tuba was until a music major asked me out, and I accepted, even though I wasn't into his lifestyle as a classical musician. I did not know what to talk about but our focus on the movie spared me, and he never found out why it was my first movie and why it was our only date.

My landlords treated me with respect and didn't ask many questions, though I'm sure they wondered about the letters and postcards that filled their mailbox each week. I mostly kept to myself unless I joined them for dinner. Sometimes they invited me to watch television in the evenings. My breakfast was simple, toast with raspberry jam and coffee, which I made myself. I had a little spot in the refrigerator for my food, which wasn't much. I survived on oatmeal raisin cookies during the day! No wonder I lost weight.

University life suited me well as a conscientious student, and time passed quickly. I was happy that God directed me to this place. Not only was the rent low, but another bonus came after I moved in. The landlady came up to me and asked, "Would you like to join us for dinner every night?"

I didn't hesitate. "Yes, of course, and thank you. How much will it cost?"

"It's included."

If I was the hugging type, I would have grabbed her in a big embrace. At least I wouldn't starve. These wonderful people probably offered dinner, as they didn't want me to mess up their kitchen. Or they pitied the awkward girl from Northwestern Ontario, though they did not know whether I could actually cook for myself.

As the weeks passed, I remembered a song in Finnish that goes something like this, "I will not walk alone one moment, but I will see Jesus beside me always." Since God was with me, when I felt lonely, I thought about Jesus, who provided for all my needs. God had been good to me and had guided my life so far.

On the second day after settling in, I heard a faint knock at my door. I pulled the doorknob slowly, wondering who it could be. A dark-skinned girl stood there and introduced herself. "I live upstairs with my roommate. I just want you to know we're here." The color of her skin amazed me because I had met no one like her before. "I'm from Jamaica. Where are you from?" she asked.

"From Thunder Bay. It's along Lake Superior in the North." For both of us, this was our first year at Western University. But best of all, we shared faith in Jesus. Again, God showed his mercy by connecting me with a Christian friend, and as a bonus, she lived in the same house.

Early in the semester, I found out I had received a grant and student loan for the academic year. I could have jumped up and down and shouted for joy, but it was not my style. One life verse I held dear was Matthew 6:33, where the Word talks about putting God first and how He will supply all my needs. No worries about finances, at least for a while. Again, I rejoiced in God's goodness. It had nothing to do with me, but His grace carried me. I didn't deserve all this. While my life as a university student was in full swing, I reflected often about Antti. What was he thinking, and would he come to Canada next summer?

My childlike faith in God brought me overwhelming peace, even though many questions remained unanswered. I knew God had more in store for me, and I wanted to understand Him intimately. I desired to be filled with the Holy Spirit's power to be a witness wherever God led me. Since I'd grown up in the Free Church and had many friends in the Pentecostal denomination, I knew about being filled with the Holy Spirit but had never experienced it. Antti also wrote about all the exciting things happening in his own life and among the youth in Finland. He often quoted the Bible verse, *"But those who wait upon the Lord shall renew their strength."* Isaiah 40:31 (NKJV) I certainly needed strength, not only for studies but for living in a new environment. He not only prayed that for himself, but for me too, as I had asked him for prayer.

God's calling seemed to be foremost on Antti's heart, as he wrote about it often, almost in every letter. He wanted to know where God would lead him after graduation. One night while living in London, I had a dream, so I wrote to him. "Everything was so mixed up, but Sofia and some other young people were there. You were having meetings, and as a result, you were physically and, perhaps, spiritually tired. I remember you were trying to hurry from one building to another. Then I came, late as usual, and found you and you looked up. It was a hilarious dream and the only dream I've had about you. And strange, I knew nothing about you, only your name."

We had corresponded for about a year, somewhat staying true to the original purpose of Antti practicing his English. At some point, our language changed to Finnish, which changed the dynamics of our relationship between teacher/student to soulmates, all platonic. We had been writing about the possibility of him coming to Canada in the summer to study English and practice oral language skills. Of course, that would not happen if he came to my hometown, as my family and friends spoke Finnish. At one point, I wrote to him that it was not time for him to come to Canada, as the work and ministry would be too difficult for a person coming from Finland looking to evangelize. In Finland, he preached in churches and schools where many young people accepted Jesus as Savior, but here he would have to look for Finnish-speaking people. We had well-established youth retreats among the churches, but many speakers preached in English, even though many of the attendees spoke Finnish at home.

Studying English would have to be accomplished in a different place. I offered to research opportunities in London, Ontario. Perhaps a farm where he could help with chores and learn Canadian customs while practicing speaking in English. Visitors could not work in Canada. That posed another obstacle to staying in Canada. He would need finances for the flight and for personal spending, even if he had free room and board. As a student, would he have money?

Planning far into the future had become an obsession for both of us. Ideas came and went as he continued to seek God's plan to seek direction toward missions. He applied to England for language school and was accepted but had to cancel it due to lack of finances. Next, he thought he would study English at the university in his hometown for the summer. That fell through. The guy was the most determined man I knew. With bulldog faith, he continued to seek the next step. I had known no one so dedicated to his calling while trying to make it happen. All the while, he kept writing me unique plans that he could pursue and asked me to pray for him. I sensed his focus and passion were totally on spreading the gospel.

Meanwhile, my university studies involved a lot of work but were enjoyable as well because I met many Christian students in the Intervarsity Club. I also attended the young adults' group at the Pentecostal Church and enjoyed the fellowship. The church was enormous, but the Sunday school class made it comfortable to meet other young adults and students from campus. Correspondence continued. But why?

7

cultural differences

THROUGHOUT MY FIRST year in London, I never shared with others about the male friend I wrote to, but I wondered what would come next for my pen pal and for me. Our views on missionary work differed so much that I questioned if we should just end it. He focused everything on Ecuador, and that's why he sought ways to learn English and, later, Spanish as well. Antti, an avid reader, devoured books like *All for Christ* by C.T. Studd and other missionary stories. One book that affected him was *Operation Auca* about the missionaries who were killed in Ecuador. I shared about reading a missionary story of two women who surrendered their lives in China, where they died a martyr's death. Reading this planted fear in my soul, the opposite of what Antti experienced.

Could I dedicate my life to God, completely trusting him without fear or doubt? Had God already ordained my destiny? I concluded I could not seek such a faith-filled life without God's strength. As a teenager, I had romanticized missions, but now realized such a life wasn't for me. As a young and immature girl, I surrendered to God. "I will go anywhere you lead me but not to Africa." Not just Africa, but any other third-world country. And yet, I corresponded with a seminary student with a mission major. Maybe I should stop writing since I wasn't interested in the same direction. Conflicting and contrasting thoughts flowed until the next letter.

Five years younger with four years of education more than me, Antti would graduate in two years. We were on different paths educationally. We were miles apart spiritually and had a stormy sea between us. He was assured in his faith and calling, while I vacillated about spiritual experiences and complained to God that I wasn't good enough to receive the Holy Spirit. I needed to be pure and righteous, which I acknowledged I was not. Besides, witnessing to unbelievers scared me, while his life was filled with street ministry, meetings, and giving talks in public schools.

What was I thinking when I visited Finland at seventeen and planned to attend Santala with Sofia? It made no sense. I hadn't even graduated from high school and had no direction. A foolish girl just wanting adventure and to get away from home. What if I had attended there? He had just started his education after a two-year exile to Sweden working at a factory, running from God's call. I probably would not have been a good influence living among other rebellious teenagers at a nearby campus to the seminary students.

Unlike many teenage girls in my circle of friends, I had not created a fantasy about marriage and family. Any dream I had about marriage would be far into the future or not at all, after I traveled the world and established a career. Would this become a reality or not?

Santala, a denominational college near the ocean in southern Finland, offered both a seminary and a vocational school, the best of both worlds, depending on one's perspective. An educational facility for young people preparing for a vocational trade or for those following God's call into the ministry. Both had their advantages. Photos of the place revealed its natural beauty. Antti often wrote about his walks along wilderness trails surrounded by tall pine trees and the ocean waves crashing on smooth rocky shores.

"I was so blessed to witness two young girls give their lives to Christ." These words often appeared in many of his letters, expressing his excitement when people were saved. However, as our writing developed into soulmate status, he also wrote about his concerns about the young students on the vocational side of the campus. While some were Christians, others were not, and some students created problems with their rebellious behavior. Antti showed compassion and kindness, no matter what happened. "My heart breaks for guys who come back to the dorm drunk. I pray for them and try to counsel them, talking with the young boys until late at night. Sometimes I'm so tired." Why did he sacrifice his time so late into the night and then have to get up early the next day? His compassion and care for others almost blew my mind. I could never measure up.

My life at the university posed unique situations. I remained oblivious to drunken parties and the campus life—a blessing. Since I didn't live on campus, there was no exposure, although I never felt tempted to party with drinking involved. I needed to be in control at all times, though life didn't always seem that way. I wanted to witness to fellow students, but fear gripped me. Back home, I belonged to the Finnish social circle, but at school among vast crowds, I didn't always feel connected. Loneliness hovered over me when I least expected it.

Keeping up with correspondence helped my sorrow on gloomy days. University was a tough place to stand up for Jesus because the educated didn't need Christ, according to popular beliefs. With the 1960s era still in full swing, the hippie movement dominated the youth culture with its drugs and rock and roll. Though I didn't take part in any of it, I often asked Antti to pray for me to overcome my shyness to share my faith.

The devil whispered in my ear, "You don't need the Holy Spirit" every time I longed to be filled with God's wisdom to help me share the gospel. I had waited a long time for the Pentecostal experience but didn't think myself good enough. I felt I didn't measure up in the holiness department. And I didn't belong to the right church. What lies the enemy planted in my young mind!

Studies mostly filled my first year at the university, along with the occasional social activity with the girls from my house. Growing up, I had no friends of color but now embraced their friendship; however, I couldn't share about my family problems back home. Antti filled the gap as a true confidant so I shared these struggles with him.

In early November, I received a disturbing letter from my sister, the one we had prayed for. She spoke of her boredom regarding life and sadness but didn't elaborate. Our parents didn't share about issues at home. I didn't know what had gone on and assumed everything was okay. I wondered if she tried to talk to my parents or the pastor. My heart broke with this knowledge, but I appreciated Antti's help with these burdens. Sadness filled my life, too. For a while, I didn't know what to do. Was she in trouble? Was a guy trying to hurt her? What was happening at home? I knew our dad should have shown his love and understanding to us kids, but he'd lacked a fatherly role model, as his own father grew up as an orphan.

Christmas break arrived, and I was happy to travel home. Glad to see my friends and family and attend my church. Life dropped back to normal, and I returned to my job at the Finnish Book Store, a job I started the summer before to earn some cash for Christmas. The owners, also immigrants, had already lived in Canada for many years, and they helped newcomers settle in Canada. If someone needed any information about jobs, housing, medical information, or places to go, my boss and his wife knew where to find it. They provided services like translation and information on agencies where people could get help. Almost like an anchor store in the middle of the Finnish cultural district, it became the hub of the Bay Street businesses where you could hear Finnish spoken on the street.

I hadn't thought of my abilities as anything but normal, but the boss apparently viewed me as an excellent worker. I started with the basics like cleaning, organizing, and lining up the shelves, but they soon promoted me to salesclerk, and then to post office clerk. As it was a few weeks before Christmas, the little post office bustled with customers trying to send snail mail to Finland or elsewhere. Multitasking became a specialty of mine, and my friendly nature helped people stay calm during stressful times.

One day, after a busy day at work, I rushed home to relax and checked the mailbox beside the door. My heart warmed. A letter mailed to my home address. We had perfected the time it took a letter to reach wherever each of us lived. I quickly stepped into my room without talking to anyone. He dated the letter December 6. The greeting, *Dear Pirkko*, appeared romantic until I read further. *Evening between two lighted candles that similarly burn on the windows of Finnish people as a remembrance of Independence Day.* Disappointed, I realized everyone burns candles on this day.

Finland signed the Declaration of Independence from Russia on December 6, 1917, but later, in 1940, surrendered a large part of southeastern Finland known as Karelia, including the city of Viipuri. Many Finns evacuated quickly, leaving their belongings behind and escaping with nothing but the clothes on their backs. Finland became a democratic modern country with a vibrant economy and a population of about 5.5 million.

I always trusted Antti to answer my questions and comment on my confusing ramblings. About my sister, he said, *I believe that there is a struggle between Jesus and the devil in Laura's life. I believe Jesus will win.* If only I had that kind of faith. He also reminded me that Jesus would baptize me with the Holy Spirit. I attended the Jesus People meetings, where I received inspiration to share my testimony of God's keeping power and faith. Their supernatural transformation as excited Jesus followers intrigued me, especially in the light of my churchy background.

In Finland, on December 24, stores closed around noon with the Declaration of Christmas Peace. While this tradition wasn't part of Canadian culture, my parents didn't shop on Christmas Eve.

Christmas dinner in our home was not the usual turkey with trimmings like Canadians. We usually had slow-baked tender ham with strong mustard, mashed potatoes with gravy, and different Finnish casseroles. Carrot, turnip, potato, and liver casserole that most kids never gained a taste for, but amazingly, I learned to like it. And for dessert, Mom always made rice pudding with either strawberry or blueberry sauce and sometimes, a prune and raisin sauce.

Our family followed the traditions of family gift-giving and dinner on Christmas Eve, and church attendance very early Christmas morning, as they did in Finland. But before all this, the house had to be clean and more or less clutter-free. The Christmas tree would be decorated with whatever we could afford or with homemade ornaments or gingerbread cookies. A few store-bought bulbs hung sparsely on pine branches.

Our father worked in the forest cutting trees for a living and brought the Christmas tree home. No fancy Hallmark Christmas tradition of a family searching for the perfect one at a tree lot. When he arrived home with a tree on top of his pickup truck, we laughed. We kids called it the Charlie Brown tree because of the sparse branches in lopsided lengths. Sometimes it looked like it had been in a dogfight. "Dad can't see the tree for the forest," I stated.

A week before Christmas, I helped Mom with some baking, which I enjoyed. Mom always kneaded the dough with muscle power since bread machines were not available. Even though a small woman, she had powerful arms. Kneading a pailful of bread dough appeared easy. Until I tried it! Whenever I had the urge to make cinnamon buns, I waited or asked Mom to prepare the dough. Her *pulla* was not as sweet, so I liked to make the cinnamon buns just to add extra sugar. Though I asked her to add more sugar, she kept her own recipe. As a frugal money manager, she knew how to stretch the penny.

"It's ready." Mom dropped the dough onto the table, sprinkled it with flour, and dug her hands into it. As she kneaded the chunk into a thick, long shape, she sang her favorite hymns. By the time she'd cut and shaped the blob of dough into separate long pieces used for braiding, she'd hummed at least a half dozen songs. She often would begin one song and then start another one without finishing the first one. *"Joulu, joulu tullut on."* She sang an old Finnish song that declared Christmas had come.

As I watched her, I asked, "I can help. Can I take this? I'll make cinnamon buns."

"Yes. Take this." Then she cut off a chunk. "I'm making the braided *pulla*, the long ones." She continued her song, twisting the long pieces into a nice braid. Picture-perfect mother-daughter bonding. Why didn't I tell her what Laura had written to me just a month earlier? That my little sister struggled with stuff. Secrets were part of growing up, but talking would have deepened our relationship, and perhaps my mother would have held my sister a little tighter. Little did I foresee the pain our family would experience on Christmas Day.

After a few hours of baking with Mom, I wrapped some presents purchased with money earned from my part-time job. Then I hid them in the closet of the bedroom I shared with my sister, Hilla.

I enjoyed Christmas Eve, especially the reading of the account of Jesus' birth. Our father took the honor to read it every year. Some Christian families sang Christmas songs, but we didn't. Gifts were mostly for the kids—whatever my parents could afford. Feeding seven kids was the primary goal in the sixties, when my father, the only breadwinner, had been unemployed for long stretches in the year.

8

leave the ninety-nine

CHRISTMAS DAY OF 1971 did not go as planned in our home. The small living room with unlit tree lights, empty boxes, and ripped wrapping paper in the corner matched my mood. Instead of the traditional candlelight service, Finnish churches held an early morning service on Christmas Day that I always attended.

My father dressed in his Sunday best brown suit with a dark-colored tie. His thick wavy hair made him look younger than middle age. Mother's Sunday dress, covered by her long winter coat, helped her appear taller than her four-feet-ten-inches. I dashed between the washroom and my room and then peeked out my bedroom window. White exhaust smoke billowed from Dad's old Chevrolet parked on the street. Not quite dressed, I heard the blast of a horn. "Wait. Hold on. Doesn't he know I will come out when ready?" I wanted to scream at him.

Without waking my sister Hilla, who slept in the same room, I dashed outside into the cold wintry morning. I pulled my hat a little tighter and shivered as I plopped onto the freezing car seat. "Funny, you're up so early," I said when I noticed the other passenger in the back. How did my brother slip past me? I needed to ask him a few questions about Laura.

After church, we arrived home. Dad looked around, frantic, and then the screaming started. We all stormed into the bedroom where my two younger sisters slept. "Where is she? Who knows where Laura went?" he yelled. Hadn't anyone noticed? She had disappeared in the night. She must have slipped out of her room off the kitchen after everyone already slept.

"We don't know," someone said. I covered my mouth so as not to yell along with the others. Chaos, crying, and yelling. Doors banged as we searched every room, closet, and the basement.

After lunch, Dad said, "We're going to look for her. Everyone, come with me." He pointed to me and said, "You stay home in case she comes back." I was glad I didn't have to go along with this madness. I imagined he spared me since I had been away from home for so long and didn't know what had gone on. Maybe Dad had a soft spot for me on this day, my twenty-first birthday. Earlier, he joked, "You're going to be an old maid."

I watched despondently as all the kids and my parents piled into the old car. I wiped my forehead and dropped onto the couch, hoping to take a nap. Peace at last. Tears remained unshed under eyelids that would not close.

Dad drove off, tires skidding on the packed snow. Where would they go? When would they be back? A memory snapped in my brain about Dad's driving lesson and his jerky footwork. I prayed he wouldn't get into an accident because of his volatile emotional state.

Though my father and mother had many faults, they were loving parents who showed how much they cared by demonstration rather than words. Driving for hours on Christmas Day around shady areas of the city revealed love in action. They left me alone and sought the one lost sheep. I waited for everyone to return. *God, if you care for us, why is this happening to our family?*

This day was special to Christians, the celebration of Jesus' birth. Why now? Why right after our family's big dinner where kids had ripped the paper off the presents and whooped it up with the few toys and clothing they received? Why on my birthday?

Our family didn't always celebrate birthdays, and in the light of all the chaos, they forgot my special twenty-first birthday. I should have just left back to London.

Why would my sister run off on Christmas Day, of all days? Why God? Words from Antti's letters popped into my mind as I lay on the couch. "Jesus will save your sister one day." I didn't know if I believed it but whispered a prayer anyway. *Lord, please keep Laura safe and bring her back home.*

I consoled myself and hoped one day to see my sister return to God. Memories crashed to the shores of my brain. She had written a few more letters but had divulged nothing about a boyfriend. I didn't know what had gone on at home in the last few months. We just didn't share stuff in our family.

My shoulders slumped at the thought of leaving home again. Hopefully, life would be better if I engrossed myself in my studies. Like burying my head in the sand. At least I wouldn't have to see or hear about the arguments and chaos. I rubbed my eyes and willed myself to cry. But no tears came. I concluded there was nothing I could do to help the strained relationships between my parents and sister.

After a few hours, a quiet knock startled me and woke me from a deep sleep. I slid off the lumpy couch and put on a brave face and approached the door. A tall blond man and a petite young woman, barely reaching his shoulders, stood with smiling faces and a bouquet wrapped in colored paper. As customary, my girlfriend always dropped by on Christmas Day. This time she came with her new husband and brought much-needed comfort and joy. Lahja had been my closest friend since grade nine and always seemed to know what to do. "Happy Birthday, and Merry Christmas." Fortunately, they didn't know what had happened a few hours ago.

"Come in. No one else is home. I'll make some coffee." I tried to sound cheery and keep most of my melancholy to myself.

"Where is everybody?" They looked around at the mess but said nothing else.

I evaded the question and guided them to the kitchen. We sat at the table with coffee and a few Christmas goodies and visited for a while until I finally found the courage to share my heart. "My parents and the others went looking for Laura. No one knows where she went. This morning we found out she'd gone, so they all went downtown."

"Didn't you go to church?" She had joined her husband's church, so I hadn't seen her this morning at the service.

"Yes, but only my parents and Osmo and I went to church."

"What's going on with your sister? Do you know anything?"

"She wrote a few sad letters to me this fall, but I don't know who she hangs out with except the girls at church." Though I suspected something bad, I didn't let on what picture evolved in my head. Only God knew. "I feel terrible because I can't communicate with her more closely."

"I'm so sorry," she said and offered compassion and prayer. I always felt Lahja was more spiritual than me, and I loved her as a sister and peace washed over me.

After they left, I curled up on the couch and daydreamed about Antti. If only he were here. We could pray together.

My parents finally came home in the evening empty-handed, without Laura. Our dad's fury had subsided by this time, and his eyes drooped toward the floor. He slipped quietly into his bedroom while I whispered to Mom, "Where did you go?"

"Downtown somewhere. Osmo wanted to go to some houses, so we tried. But no one had seen her." As her custom, she divulged little information about anything, and we each retreated to our bedrooms. Loneliness gripped my heart, as it seemed nobody cared.

I often poured my worries out onto paper to my confidant, from the comfort of my bedroom while sitting at my desk watching the trees sway like the mixed thoughts in my brain. Some conversations had to be imagined, while others would have to wait until we were face-to-face.

"Do you know what I think?" I wanted to ask Antti.

And he would answer, "No, I can't know unless you tell me. It's so hard because we're not together."

Why didn't he phone? Probably because he had no money for overseas calls. It'd been over a year of correspondence, so I'd grown more confident about sharing my inner conflicts. "Well, I hate my home sometimes. It's so painful to watch all that goes on. At least I'm not in the middle of every crisis that happens. I know it's insensitive, but sometimes I just don't care anymore."

Laura's behavior had been a source of discouragement for all of us so his words would encourage me. "You will see your sister join God's family one day."

"Okay, if you say so! Right now, I'm not sure."

"Jesus will answer in time. Nothing is impossible with God."

"Wouldn't it be nice if we had no cares of the world? I'm sorry. I shouldn't burden you with everything. Though I don't know you very well, I know you will try to understand."

"I'm happy if I can help you. I don't have all the answers but Galatians 6:2 talks about carrying each other's burdens. I've had my own struggles but not so much in our family."

Did anyone else have the same issues we had? I doubt it. *What is wrong with my family and this world?*

9

mexico on my mind

AFTER THE CHRISTMAS holidays, I traveled back to London knowing Laura had returned home safely, and my life seemed full as I looked forward to living away where I buried my nose into the books and attended classes. I typed essays for fellow students for some pocket money.

My emotions grew conflicted regarding Antti's continued advice about seeking the Lord for guidance for the future. Hadn't I made my decision? I studied at university to pursue a career in education. Was he reading something into our pen pal relationship that I was missing? *I can't read between the lines.* After all, we had no obligations to each other outside of language practice. *Well, maybe there's more to this soulmate connection?*

Then a bombshell of unexpected news arrived. Though he wrote a lot about his desire to study English abroad, which we discussed in many letters, Thunder Bay was not the place to learn English.

I imagined Antti sitting in his room, studying and writing about his plans, and us having this conversation.

"I had a very busy Christmas holiday. I worked at the meat plant and traveled to a mission conference at the college during New Year's."

"How was it?"

"There were over 140 young people from all over Finland including mission candidates and students. We watched the film Näin Aucojen Rukoilevan, *Saw Auca's Pray* (1963). My heart warmed with unexplainable joy." Every time he mentioned Ecuador in his letter, he added something about me seeking God's direction.

"As you know, I had a sad Christmas Day, my birthday. Is your older brother planning to move to Canada?"

"Yes, he's talking about it and asking me questions."

Then without warning, he revealed he had made a plan to come to Canada. "I booked a flight to Toronto, hoping to find a place to stay for the summer. I wrote to a pastor there asking if he could arrange for me to stay with an English-speaking family."

"You mean in Toronto and not Thunder Bay? That would make sense."

"If you have any other ideas let me know," he said.

"Okay. There are many farms around the London area. Maybe try to find one there. At least it's away from all the Finnish populations."

Several weeks later, everything changed for Antti again. He would come to Thunder Bay instead.

"What? You're coming to my hometown? You certainly won't learn English."

"Yes, I wrote to the pastor in Thunder Bay, and he arranged everything for me, even a ride from Toronto to Thunder Bay with a Finnish business owner. Isn't that great?" I could almost feel his excitement with my heartbeat.

Mixed feelings swirled as my opinions changed day by day. On one hand, it excited me we could finally have those conversations in person. But why now? It didn't seem to fit any of my summer plans.

I prolonged the next letter for almost a month as I contemplated our situation and ignored writing about his plan. Instead, my letters detailed my daily activities. Studying for tests. Attending various services at Anglican and Pentecostal churches and Jesus People gatherings. Opinions about things, mainly religion. How the testimonies of various Jesus People stirred my "church girl" heart. I had never heard of the depths of darkness these young people were saved from.

London
February 20, 1972

Dear Antti,

…Many thanks for your last letter and the beautiful postcard…I thank the Lord for a friend.

…As you might have noticed, I'm quite critical and frustrated at the relationships between the different churches… Yes, it's true what you said about lifting your eyes upon the Lord Jesus Christ. I wish and pray I could always be able to do that and not look at people.

…You know something? Laura has changed so much lately, although she has not yet yielded completely. It's wonderful to hear that she admits…the devil has his tricks, but in the end, God will be victorious. Isn't that right? God has been working among young people everywhere. A

guy in my English class has found the Lord Jesus Christ. Also, two other
guys who used to live in my parent's rental house were saved just before
Christmas, and I heard excellent reports from our church back home.
May God be with you in all you do.
Sincerely,
Pirkko

Still uptight about Antti coming to Thunder Bay, I determined to make travel plans to Mexico for the summer. My Spanish professor told us about a language studies program where students live with a local family to immerse themselves in the culture and practice language skills. I loved to travel and learn the Spanish language. Adventure and education seemed like a good idea. Two girls from the class were interested as well.

I suggested this same idea to Antti for his language studies. What happened? Was God in this? *Why is he coming to Thunder Bay?* Totally surprised by his plan, my mind worked overtime planning how he could benefit from coming to our city. The only way he could improve his English was through a program provided by the government for new immigrants. Perhaps he could stay with a Canadian family. Or not come! My brain reverberated, and my emotions rolled like a skier meandering on fresh powder.

What did Antti think of my intentions? Though I loved the idea of Mexico, I added this to my letter: "I don't know if the Lord is leading, but if He doesn't want me to go, He can change my plans."

I imagined what crossed Antti's thoughts about his coming to Canada this summer. His faith would probably be tested. And what did he think the purpose of this trip would be? Our church planned its tenth anniversary celebrations on the weekend of June 9-11, and he could be a guest speaker if he arrived for that.

He wrote, "I heard about a small group of Finnish believers in Sudbury. I would like to stop there on the way if it's possible."

We could consider the Finnish immigrants in Canada a mission field if he saw it that way. It wasn't Ecuador but a ministry among a people who needed Jesus as well. There would be no language barriers, and visiting Finnish Canadian churches would give a glimpse of life here.

Antti's visit, like all others from Finland, would be welcomed with warm hospitality. People viewed it as a treat to hear preachers from the old country. Though fluent in Finnish, my place culturally seemed at odds, pulled in two directions. I lived and worked with immigrants in the church who spoke very little English, while not fully immersed in the Canadian culture. Having a young student minister to our small congregation excited me, probably as much as it excited Antti, but for different reasons.

Our correspondence for the past two years bordered on friendliness, platonic at most, and inconsistent between the lines. *Was there something?*

One day after service, our pastor came to talk to me when I was almost out the door. "I've made arrangements with a Christian couple in the country where Antti could stay. All he needs to do is help with some chores on the farm. He would have to speak English since they're not Finn." I turned my head and smiled tentatively until I realized what he was saying.

"How did you know about him coming?" I hadn't divulged about Antti's plans. The pastor cared for the church and my comings and goings and would advise if needed. But I didn't always talk about what was happening in my life, especially about my correspondence with Antti.

He smiled and said, "Antti wrote to me. And I already arranged a ride for him from Toronto."

I mumbled something and walked out to the parking lot. An older lady noticed me and approached with a mischievous smile. She touched my arm lightly. "I heard the pastor telling you about arranging a place for someone to stay. I heard a guest is coming to Canada. Is it someone I know?"

Marvelous how quickly my personal business became common knowledge. "Yes. Another speaker from Finland." I left it at that and strolled away.

In his next letter, Antti confirmed this plan as God's guidance in his life. He had grown familiar with our church through our correspondence and by writing to Sofia and the pastor.

Sometimes jitters shook in the pit of my stomach, while other times I hummed a song of praise to God. Soon, my soulmate friend would visit Thunder Bay. Unbelievable how this all came to be! I had never seriously dreamed of this. Writing letters had led to misunderstandings. And now that we were about to meet in person, I wondered what he thought of me and everything I had divulged. My throat tingled and heat rose to my neck.

I wrote these words before his arrival: "It's going to be a treat to have someone come from the homeland to minister to our little congregation. God will bless your ministry here. I know."

I knew I may have fed Antti's ego too much when he responded, "Sometimes I feel your vision of me makes me too good, and how God leads me, though it's true that God has guided me supernaturally often. But it's not about me, but His grace."

I continued, "I believe your love for God's work will be a real blessing here and people will receive God's love."

Antti offered gratitude to God that he would be in His will and nothing would be greater than to be involved in the Lord's work. I felt a little envious, though I admired his love for God.

His last letter before arrival to my hometown.

Lahti
May 24, 1972

Dear Pirkko,
…I know there is some purpose in my trip because everything has been so well-prepared. Hopefully, I can share with you what God has given me. Do not expect too much from me to avoid any disappointments. Sometimes fear sneaks into my heart that I won't be able to give what's expected of me. I wait with anticipation for all that I will experience over there: your summer camps and the other activities you have.
Jesus Christ, my most loved in the world.
Greetings,
Antti

By early spring, most of the people in our church knew I had been writing to a guy at the denomination's seminary. I braced for an onslaught of teasing. They did not know about our relationship and had me married already. One senior lady saw a dream of me in a wedding dress, and others joked about it, but my dad declared me a spinster at age twenty-one.

About the teasing, Antti wrote, "I don't care, since they don't know about our friendship or how we related to each other for the last two years." This visit would provide an opportunity to meet in person, to have actual conversations, to avoid misinterpretations common when writing. We had so much to talk about, missions being one of the most important topics, along with my education.

God also directed my next step for the summer. With an excellent resume with the completion of first-year university in the Secretarial Science program, I picked up a high-paying government summer job with the Ministry of Natural Resources. My vacation had taken shape, and unfortunately, the Mexico trip fell by the wayside. Was I sorry for this? Disappointed, but it should be a splendid summer.

In my last letter before his arrival, I ended with these words: "I'm wishing you the best in everything, and may the Lord be everything in everything. Greetings, Pirkko."

10

first impressions of canada

BUILDINGS APPEARED LIKE matchboxes below, though the skyscrapers reached dozens of stories high into the Toronto landscape. What a sight! Mesmerized, his eyes glued to the scuffed-up glass window of the jumbo jet, Antti's heart flowed with gratitude to his Savior. The long flight from Helsinki to Iceland for refueling, and then to Toronto, tired him, but he kept his eyes on the amazing view.

The Suomi-Seura charter flight landed at Toronto International Airport on Friday, June 3, 1972. After passengers disembarked the airplane and filed into the busy airport, Antti surveyed the location intently to beat the crowd to the baggage area. He followed signs above the corridors, and he spotted a water fountain nearby and stopped for a drink. Next, he stepped into the men's washroom. After taking care of business, he was ready to tackle the next phase and find his way to the immigration department. He understood enough English to know the direction from reading the signs. He scurried through the crowded corridors with a small flight bag strapped to his shoulder and a handbag that bulged with his few belongings and gift bags of the famous Finnish coffee, *Kultamokka*.

If he had fears of any kind, he kept them to himself. There was no time to be nervous, as he was on a mission to meet his connection. How would he recognize the man from the thousands of people, as no one had provided any distinguishing details, not even a photo?

After two hours, Antti hurried toward the passenger pickup area to meet his contact. A stranger to him, but a brother in Christ. Karl, a recent immigrant himself, lived in Toronto and was eager to help accommodate a Christian brother from Finland. As the escalator slid downward, Antti peered through the massive crowd of people. Would Karl hold up a sign? Then, as if by a divine appointment, a middle-aged man with brown hair, glasses, and a smile approached. He appeared to look for someone.

"*Oletko Karl?*" Antti asked.

"Yes, that's me, and you are Antti?" Karl's eyes twinkled like stars in a dark night.

The pastor planned for the connection with Arvo, a business owner from Thunder Bay, to provide the ride to Thunder Bay. Arvo always stayed at Karl's home when visiting Toronto for business. These wonderful believers had prepared Antti's visit in advance. God had provided.

A friendly man, Karl insisted they visit Niagara Falls, the world-famous waterfall and a honeymooners' capital of Canada, the next day, no matter Antti's jetlag. Before driving to Niagara Falls, they toured Toronto's downtown, where he witnessed the early part of the construction of the CN Tower. What was the purpose of a building so tall with an elevator on the outside just to experience the thrill of the ride? Antti had not imagined the enormous size of the city. Roads full of cars whizzed by on multiple lanes of traffic. Would he ever get used to this? How could a farm boy from Central Finland experience such a marvel? An experience beyond any dreams!

After a restful night, it was time to hit the road and bid farewell to his gracious host family in Toronto. Another adventure to experience awaited him—a sixteen-hour road trip with a strange man. Though Antti traveled in Europe many times, this was different. The sheer number of miles of road never seemed to end once they were on the highway.

"How far is Thunder Bay?" Antti asked his driver after a few hours.

"You sit in the car for another three days and three nights, and you'll get there," Arvo jested with a serious face, but within a few seconds, Antti caught on as he remembered Pirkko wrote about the distance in terms of hours and not days.

"What do you mean? I thought it was only a day's drive." Antti couldn't figure out if the guy was serious or not so he put on his poker face.

"No, it's actually a two-day drive if you stay overnight in the Soo."

"What's Soo? I've never heard of it. I saw Sault Ste. Marie on the map."

"It's a small city halfway between Toronto and Thunder Bay. We can stop there for gas and get some *kentoki siken*."

"What's that?"

After a few minutes in deep thought, Arvo explained, "Chicken fried in grease. You'll like it. Everyone does."

"Oh! I like chicken but we don't eat a lot of chicken in Finland."

Arvo turned toward him with a slight smirk and asked, "Do you have a girlfriend?" Then he pulled into a small gas station in the middle of nowhere. Antti wondered why he asked about a girl when the topic had never come up anywhere, not even back home, but dismissed it as a rumor.

"No girlfriend," Antti answered.

The driver cut the engine and slipped out. "Time for a pee break," he said. "Next stop is four hours away."

Hunger pangs curled in Antti's stomach, and he could hardly wait for the chicken. Was he ever glad Karl's wife insisted they take a bag lunch to hold them over until they reached the Soo.

The road trip seemed to go on and on, with no end in sight. Then Arvo suddenly announced after a long stretch of silence, "We're going to drive right through to Thunder Bay, with no overnight stopping. It's only sixteen hours in total. Can you make it?"

"Sure. As long as we get the *kentoki siken*." That's how he pronounced it, in Finglish. Antti nodded off several times, but his naps couldn't last too long, as Arvo would interrupt his solitude with banter about something trivial.

They passed a small town called Blind River and stopped at the only traffic light. Arvo pressed the accelerator, but the old half-passenger-half-cargo van only lumbered on. It gradually picked up speed. Finally, they turned into a small parking lot near a plaza with unfamiliar businesses. As soon as they opened the door to the restaurant, the smell of grease accosted his nose. His saliva glands already set in motion with anticipation, he followed his driver into the little diner, where a few tables sat empty along the window. Arvo ordered a bucket of chicken in his broken English. "We need nothing else because after you eat this good chicken, you will be full but thirsty."

"Good. Are we going to sit down?"

"No. We have to go. That's why it comes in a bucket, so you can take it with you."

Antti followed his companion to the vehicle and retrieved a bottle of water from his bag as he wondered how they were going to eat with no plates or utensils. Without uttering a word, he watched the man take a chunk of chicken with his fingers and bite into it. Grease oozed onto the guy's chin while he chewed the juicy, crisp piece, moaning in between bites and whispering *hyvä*. After biting into the first piece of a breast, Antti understood why this chicken should be savored. Sweet, salty, and savory. Greasy. Like something out of this world. He fell in love with Canadian fast food.

Arvo smiled in satisfaction after he'd swallowed his last bite and licked his fingers. "The greasiness makes it so good. And the secret spices."

Antti ate in silence, marveling at the taste, then made his declaration. "Yes, so good. I like this."

THE NEXT MORNING, Antti rotated his legs to the edge of the bed, prepared to get up, when something caught his attention. Shocked and dazed, he turned and found a blond head peeking out from under the covers at the far corner of the room in a single bed. With wide eyes, he stared. *This couldn't be!* They arrived after midnight. He did not know to whose house Arvo dropped him. Jetlagged and overly tired, he'd climbed into his bed and slept a few hours. *Who's this little girl?* As he processed his thoughts, he bounced to his feet, grabbed his clothes from the chair, and walked out of the room to the bathroom.

Through a miscommunication, his first night in Thunder Bay turned out to be in the wrong house. Always the jokester, Arvo dropped his guest at a young family's house with no extra bedroom instead of at the prearranged destination. The father, an elder of the church, invited him to stay the night. A good sport, Antti told the parents he slept well and thanked them, but he wanted to get to the right house.

The Ranta family lived in a large old two-story house on the same street as the church. It would be his stopover until he arrived at the prearranged farm for his summer stay. The aroma of coffee accosted him as he walked in the front door while he glanced around the living room— simple but homey. Sulo and his wife were pillars of the church where they served in many ministries. Their two teenage sons still lived at home, while two other adult children had already married, a son and a daughter.

"How was your trip?" Sulo asked and took Antti's coat to hang it in the closet.

Antti smiled. "Interesting. That Arvo is a character."

The matron of the house, a tall slender middle-aged woman, worked in the kitchen and prepared breakfast while her husband sat in the chair opposite Antti. As the man of the house, Sulo's demeanor oozed kindness and compassion, but he didn't engage in small talk. He went right to the business at hand. "Our pastor just resigned and moved out of town. He's planning to go to the mission field. So, your visit here came at the right time."

Antti's first impression of him felt warm and friendly, and he took a liking to this fatherly man right away. "What do you mean?"

"You might have to fill in for a while before we get another pastor to take over."

"Hmmm. Oh, I don't know. I'm just a student, and I hope to attend English language school here." He crossed and uncrossed his legs. When Sulo suggested they visit the farm to see the place before he moved in later in the week, he agreed. The gravity of speaking at the anniversary meetings already weighed heavily on his mind.

Antti noticed the drab gray barns and other outbuildings along the gravel road as they drove in the country. Dilapidated buildings stuck out like a sore thumb along the edge of white pine trees mixed with some birch. So different from Finland, where the barns were red, and the yards were kept clean, free of garbage and broken-down machines and vehicles. In Finland, they even cleared the underbrush along the highways.

Antti grew up on a farm, where he lived until the age of sixteen, so he expected a pleasant experience of looking after animals and working the fields with the farmer. As a child, he named his own cow, almost like a pet—not like cats, of course, but just to distinguish his cow from his four siblings' cows. He learned to clean the barn of manure and waste and to organize the food bins for the animals. His mother taught him how to milk the cows and feed the horses. His father and two brothers worked in the hayfields in the summer and logged in the winter. Familiar with farm life, he wondered if this experience would be suitable. By the looks of the dismal scenery along the way, Antti lowered his expectations, declaring that he could do this, more to himself than to anyone else.

Lost in his thoughts, he was startled by the horn as they arrived at a location that looked nothing like his imagination. "Here we are."

An older woman opened the heavy door. "Come in. We've been waiting for you." She smiled widely and welcomed her guests with open arms.

If first impressions proved true, then Antti viewed this place as depressing. The unkempt surroundings irked his analytical mind, but he concluded they may have health or other issues. The woman with gray hair asked them to sit at the kitchen table. "Would you like some coffee or tea?"

To be polite, they both answered in the affirmative for coffee. After all, what Finn doesn't drink the stuff? It wouldn't be polite if they didn't at least sit down and chat with the woman. They found out her friend was a missionary who'd lived in Ecuador. Just what he needed. A real live missionary from Ecuador, the country he planned to move to when ready. If this house was any sign of primitive life, it didn't feel appealing. Then again, missionaries sacrifice the comforts of their home and country in order to spread the good news about Jesus.

Soon, the percolator stopped bubbling. She poured the coffee into mugs and placed them in front of the men and handed each a spoon. The cream and a glass container of sugar were already on the table. Antti wondered what he should do with the spoon after he stirred the coffee. No saucer. He watched Sulo and followed his example, licked the spoon, and placed it on the not-so-clean table. It was a little watery, but coffee all the same. His choice would have been dark roasted and strong, but not bitter enough to be espresso. Again, out of politeness, he said nothing to his hostess nor his friend.

"Thank you for the coffee. Should we look around?" Sulo asked.

The woman stood and scurried around the kitchen before heading toward the back door. "Yes. First, let's go to the basement where your room will be."

Antti and Sulo followed her down some steep wooden stairs that creaked like a ghost in the wind. Every step seemed to vibrate with warning sounds it may break. Antti couldn't believe his eyes as they landed on the concrete floor. Boxes and old furniture filled one corner of the basement. They walked down a narrow hallway lit only by a bare low-wattage lightbulb in the ceiling.

The door to the bedroom scratched the floor as she opened it. "Here's where you'll sleep."

Antti watched as Sulo's eyes wandered from side to side inconspicuously. The metal bed's mattress sagged in the middle like a hammock. If the concrete floors weren't dismal enough, the concrete walls forced a cold sweat. He submitted to God's will long ago, but could he live here or did God test him? Reality ensnared him. Was he cut out to become a missionary after all? Or perhaps this was the place where he would learn to live a simple life while honing his English and serving at the church. After all, it was only for the summer.

Heavy footsteps from upstairs nudged Antti's ears. The woman explained, "Excuse me. It's my husband. He just came back from the store."

As soon as she left the room, Sulo turned around with slumped shoulders, as if ready to find the nearest exit. His forehead crinkled. Antti could almost see thoughts of escape burst out of his skin. Before they found the stairs, Sulo whispered, "You can't stay here. Let's go back to my house."

They said their goodbyes to the woman and her husband, who looked a little bewildered that they left so soon.

They rode back to the Ranta residence in silence. What could have been an excellent opportunity to be immersed in Canadian culture turned disastrous. What now? Where would he live? His pen pal's family had no room in their small house. With a new resolve, Antti comforted himself with God, who would continue to provide as he'd done on this trip so far.

After he settled into a cozy room on the second floor of the Rantas' house, clothes organized on hangers and in the chest of drawers, he lay on the comfortable bed before getting ready for the weekend. He focused on prayer and preparation of sermons for the upcoming anniversary meetings, choosing to remain in seclusion.

The next morning, the clanking of dishes from the kitchen and quiet conversation between the elder man and his wife traveled into his room. He might overthink it, but how he wished he could stay with this family. The smell of bacon filled the air as he dressed and completed his morning routine.

Without being invited, Antti strolled into the kitchen for breakfast. Bright sun filled the room through the tall window. After a brief prayer and a sip of coffee, he dug into the fried egg and picked up his toast. He eyed the homemade strawberry jam, his favorite. It would be good on toast. But mixing the sweetness with the salty would be interesting. "Try it. It tastes good." His hosts smiled.

Antti followed their example and spread a good helping of jam onto his toast and cut up the bacon with a knife. "This is good," he agreed after his first bite.

The conversation veered into the business of his accommodations. Sulo assured him it would be best for him to stay with them. His wife confirmed it with a nod. "Yes, you can stay here since we have the room. You have the bedroom upstairs, and you can come and go as you please," Sulo said.

A burden lifted. Antti rejoiced that he would live with these wonderful kind people for the summer. "Thank you so much."

After breakfast, Sulo stood with a smile and asked, "What are you planning to do today? If you need a ride, I can drive you. Are you going to visit anyone today?"

Thoughts of his friend passed through his mind, but he must stay on course. He could hardly believe how God's goodness surrounded him. "I'm going to spend time preparing for the meetings. And later I would like to see the church building."

If he hadn't agreed to become the speaker at the church's special meetings, he would have met up with Pirkko, but he imagined he would see her at the meetings on Friday night. Unless she changed her mind and flew to Mexico. Hopefully not.

11

is he going to ask me out?

THE HEAVY DOOR TO the familiar building almost crashed on me as I pulled the metal handle too hard then hoped life would stand still to avoid embarrassment. Arriving late would not look good on a resume, especially this one. After all, I had not yet met Antti, who arrived in the city on Tuesday, three days earlier, and I was eager to connect in person.

The little clapboard church at the junction of John Street and Empress Avenue filled with expectant souls. On this sunny, cool summer Friday evening, the Finnish immigrant congregation celebrated ten years of God's faithfulness. I slipped in inconspicuously and claimed a seat on a bench three rows from the podium. As the sanctuary could hold only about a hundred people, the alcove-like platform was positioned close to the audience. An old piano stood on the right, and the brown wooden pulpit with a white cross sat on the opposite side. Had the walls been a lighter color, it would create a more vibrant mood, as compared to the dark panels the congregants had to look at Sunday after Sunday. But today was different. They added a colorful flower arrangement to the ledge behind the altar along with the usual greenery.

After the preliminary hymns and announcements, a young preacher stood at the podium with no air of superiority. Quite the opposite. A friendly, honest face with a smile as wide as the ocean. With piercing eyes, he appeared to be observing the people in front of him.

By the end of the evening, Antti's passion for God filtered through his sermon, and his seriousness radiated through his command of the Scriptures. I observed his demeanor as he expounded on the Word of God, but nothing stuck to my brain.

My initial observation of his presence at the pulpit remained foggy mixed with scattered emotions. We had not yet spoken as my thoughts wandered to our two years of correspondence. What had I revealed about myself? That's probably why his eyes shifted elsewhere. He didn't seem to notice me and needed to concentrate.

Though we had a platonic relationship, a knot formed in my stomach as I contemplated things, wondering what could happen and if something more might develop between us. I attended the first night of the weekend services but only talked with him briefly. I thought it was odd that he didn't acknowledge me publicly during the three nights. He seemed so passionate about preaching that we didn't connect much. Was he nervous? Perhaps I was a distraction, so he avoided me—

even after the service—and rushed off with the Rantas while I positioned myself by the door. At least we had brief conversations about the church.

Was he really that cute close-up? Or was it my imagination that I had a crush on this guy behind the pulpit? Antti carried himself with honor and authority, dressed in a dark suit and clean white shirt. A beige and blue tie reminded me of tradition. This "uniform" would be my cue. *I prefer a well-dressed man.* I wanted to talk to him—just like everyone else, it seemed. But when he smiled at me from across the aisle one evening, my heart pumped an extra beat.

I observed as people swarmed around him. He appeared comfortable chatting with strangers. When he finally approached me after the last night of the conference with that wide smile, I perceived his authenticity. The rain had pelted the roof during the service, and the downpour kept the temperature cool. Only nine degrees Celsius on this Sunday in the middle of June. Not unusual for Thunder Bay, a city with a lot of thunder and lightning. *Perhaps I'll ask if he wants a ride.*

"Hello. Sorry I haven't talked to you much. I had to focus on my preaching, as this was difficult to be on for three days in a row and speaking to a new audience." He stood in front of me with his Bible in his hands, as if ready to leave.

"That's okay. I see," I lied. How could I understand? Though aware of his singlemindedness through the letters, I did not know how it worked in practice. Now I observed it in real time. His love for the Lord engulfed his thoughts, probably day and night.

"Tomorrow, I plan to go to the language school to apply for the summer course if Sulo drives me."

"I would offer you a ride, except I have to work. I'm sure he's happy to give you a ride." My eyes wandered to see who was around and kept my enthusiasm inside.

Antti's lean body and sparkly eyes caught my attention as he moved closer to me at the back of the church after most folks had already left. *Is this guy going to ask me out or not?* Now he'd be focused on summer school. *Does he realize the proper etiquette for a guy to ask a girl?* If he said nothing, I decided to be brave and suggest something.

After we talked for a few minutes about the service and people, I mustered up enough courage when I didn't see Sulo or his wife nearby. They must have gone home and left him to walk. Or was it a setup?

"Do you want a ride? To your place, I mean."

"Thanks for the offer, but I think I'll walk." I guess he wasn't interested in seeing the town…or me.

The next day, on Monday, he called my house and told me about his experience at the language school. I could feel his excitement as he relayed his acceptance to full-time studies. He would be in class Monday to Friday from nine to three. Sounded wonderful. I worked the same shift, except until four-thirty.

"When do you start?"

"Tomorrow morning. And I can take the bus, so I won't need to bother anyone for a ride."

"That's good. What are you doing after supper? I could drop by the house tomorrow evening." I invited myself but didn't have the nerve for anything more.

"Nothing. I'll stay there and maybe go for a walk. Yes, come over. I'm sure they will be happy to see you as well."

The Rantas were close friends with our family, so I was used to visiting them, especially since their daughter, Lahja, was my girlfriend. I had been her maid of honor at her wedding over two years earlier.

On Tuesday evening Antti answered the door dressed in casual clothes, dark pants, and a short-sleeved collar shirt. He grabbed his jacket, and we headed out after greeting his hosts.

"Where do you want to go?" I asked, ignorant of the fact he was the tourist. I fidgeted with my keys and hoped my nervousness didn't show.

"You can take me to whatever places you want. I don't have a preference since I'm here for the first time."

I had my brother's monstrous old clunker that swayed like a boat on the waves. The temperatures had been cooler the previous week. So, I had on my thick jacket but soon had to open the buttons as heat rose to my neck. He didn't open the door for me because it wasn't a date. That kind of etiquette wasn't needed. I took the driver's seat like a pro, and Antti scooted into the passenger seat, staying comfortably close to the window, a respectable distance between us.

"I'm going to drive you around a few places just so you can see the sights a bit. Is that okay?" Of course, he would agree. Why would I even ask?

The first place I wanted to show him was the famous, most-visited lookout. Hillcrest Park faced the largest freshwater lake in the world, Lake Superior. It's one of the five Great Lakes bordered by Canada and the United States. Deep and cold, the lake features the Sleeping Giant landmass off the shore, often a highlight in travel magazines and photographed frequently by tourists. Though the park itself boasts massive flower gardens, we moved on. Surely he wasn't interested in flowers. When darkness fell, after ten o'clock on summer nights, many lovers parked there.

We talked as we drove to the next place. "How did you like the park?"

"It was interesting. The view of the lake was nice. Did you say it's a famous tourist attraction?"

"Yes. I rarely go there. No reason to. It's also used for wedding photos." I turned the corner and down a small hill toward Bay Street.

After we parked in front of a large historic building called *Hoito*, he rolled down his window. "What's that? It has a Finnish name."

"It's the Finnish labor temple with a restaurant in the basement. The word *hoito* means "care" because the staff supplies the customers' food needs. They even make bag lunches for the men. There's a long history behind it, but let's go inside and have some coffee and we can talk."

I took the lead, and we descended the concrete stairs to the lower area. Light wooden tables with chairs filled the room. Barstools stood on the left side, with glass cabinets across from the counter. Before we found our seats, I joked about the antique weight scale in the lobby. "People need to weigh themselves before going in and again when leaving. The food is so fattening and the portions are piled a mile high. You'll put on five pounds in just one sitting."

"Really?" Antti's nose scrunched as he peered into my face.

"Yeah. Wait until you see the steaks. They're an inch thick and cover the plate. Yuck! I don't eat a lot of meat. Do you?"

"Yes. We eat a lot of meat and potatoes in Finland."

Since it was close to the supper hour, locals and tourists alike filled the place. We found a table in the corner. The rumble of voices reached my ears as I scanned the room for anyone I might know. Thunder Bay, a small town compared to the cities in Southern Ontario, made it easy to run into familiar people.

Antti placed his hands on the table and crossed his fingers and watched as I craned my neck. "I already ate. I'll have coffee."

Satisfied to find no familiar faces in the crowd, I turned to him. "Okay. They have the best homemade pies."

A blonde, middle-aged server approached us with a notepad. She smiled and spoke. "What can I get you?"

"My friend just arrived from Finland and hasn't tried your pies. What kind do you have tonight?"

Her face lit up as she looked at him. "*Kiva. Tervetuloa.*" Nice. Welcome.

From the corner of my eye, I gazed as his shoulders and back straightened at her perfect Finnish pronunciation. Antti enjoyed chatting and wanted to connect with immigrants. I took a deep breath to savor the moment and kept my eyes on his profile while they conversed. His friendly, composed manners with people increased my heartrate. He finally agreed to try apple pie for the first time in his life.

12

meeting the family

WE ENJOYED PLEASANT conversation while visiting
the Hoito Restaurant. I should have talked more about my
family instead of city sites, but I was excited for him to
experience my hometown and talk about the Finnish
immigrants and how they affected the city with their hard work.
Antti probably surmised I would be private in person but more
vulnerable in writing as I had shown through confiding in him
about worries over my sister's issues.

We made plans to visit my home on Saturday so he
phoned our house to remind me to pick him up. It wasn't
strange for my father to answer the phone and remain silent for
the longest time, as if waiting for the caller to say something.

I could only hear one side of the conversation, and Antti probably introduced himself politely. When no one said anything, I'm sure Antti had to think he'd dialed the wrong number. In Finland, when anyone answers the phone, they say their last name. "Rytkonen residence" for example.

Finally, after almost a minute, Dad spoke his first name in a quiet voice. That my dad only replied with his given name wasn't odd for our family, any more than his way of waiting for the caller to speak first.

I just hoped he didn't think badly of my father for his lack of courtesy, shown by not asking me to come to the phone. I'm sure the silence unsettled Antti. Since he operated heavy machinery for his job, Dad could be hard of hearing. Finally, he called me. "Antti wants to talk to you." Antti asked if I could pick him up to visit our house.

I parked my father's old Chevy on the street in front of our house, but not before grazing the grass on the curb. I looked down at the steering wheel and covered my face with my hands. Hopefully the hub caps remained in place. I didn't want to deal with it in front of my friend. The moment was too important to ruin the day. It was my first time bringing home my almost-boyfriend, though they'd met at church on the weekend and the previous Thursday evening.

I wondered who would be home this Saturday morning. Our usual lively bunch of kids would override any schoolyard brawl if the situation warranted it. I hoped and prayed he would see us as a loving decent family. I left the house earlier in the morning, so I didn't know who remained. It wasn't uncommon for us kids to leave the house and return home late in the evening. In the 1960s, families didn't worry about kids being out alone. The neighborhood, though mostly on the poor side of town, posed no threat, and all the kids nearby were our friends. We lived on one of the most revered streets of the city, called Winnipeg Avenue, but our small house stood on the south end of the street at the bottom of a hill that separated us from the classic immaculate homes to the north. We lived on the wrong side of the tracks by some standards, though it didn't bother us.

I fiddled with the handle and opened the car door. I cringed as the door banged louder than I thought. Antti stepped onto the grassy boulevard from the passenger side.

"This is it. Not much to look at. The house needs a good paint job. Hope it gets done someday." I looked away as we stepped onto the concrete stairs. "When they installed the stairs a few years ago, a handrail wasn't in the budget. I have to be careful so I don't fall off the edge when I'm in a hurry, which is most of the time." I noticed from the corner of my eye a little blond head peeking out the large front window. My six-year-old brother, curious to see our visitor.

Antti waited patiently as I opened the screen door. I watched his expression. He looked happy to be there but said nothing. I didn't need to knock because I lived there, at least for the summer. Besides, we didn't lock the doors, not even at night. The door opened before I put my hand on the knob. My dad stood in silence with a big grin on his face. I turned to Antti as he stepped back and appeared a little apprehensive.

"Let's go in," I said.

The living room looked half decent this morning, as I'd made sure we—mostly me—had cleaned it before I brought Antti for his first visit. After all, we ought to make a good impression on the new intern pastor of the church. I'd demanded the kids take their shoes and toys away so the appearance of a clutter-free house would impress our guest. The nature of our relationship still up in the air, I felt nervous.

The brown three-seater couch, usually filled with stuff, now looked inviting, and the old mustard color vinyl recliner in the corner, though torn at the arms, stood the test of abuse as the kids rummaged on it. Antti appeared a clean and organized man, quite the opposite of my father, who worked hard physical labor. His fingernails were often black from the grease and grime from fixing his machines and his hands calloused.

Mother strolled into the living room as we moved away from the doorway. Her relaxed appearance and smiling face showed her raised cheekbones. Her dark hair flowed around her ears, close to her shoulders, grazing her short neck. Mom was confident but a little shy when introduced to strangers.

Dad met us at the door. "This is Antti. You've already met at the church. Sorry we didn't come earlier in the week, but it's been a crazy time. Antti started his English classes on Tuesday, and I haven't seen him much, except for Tuesday evening, when we went to Hillcrest Park and Hoito."

"Glad you're here. We were waiting for you." Mom gestured to the kitchen.

"Nice to meet you," Antti said and looked around as if wondering what to do next. I noticed his gentlemanly manners and appreciated his kindness to everyone.

The kitchen, at the back of the house, was the place for gathering with visitors, and thankfully, clean as well. No dishes in the sink. The floor shone and a lingering scent of pine and chlorine hung in the air. Antti followed me to the table as Mom moved to the sink and poured water into the Pyrex percolator and carefully placed the apparatus inside. Mom measured several spoonfuls of coffee grounds into the basket and lifted the pot onto the stove element. I'm not sure how many of those glass coffee pots broke in our household. Probably a few. Dad, as usual, took the seat at the head of the table.

"Make it strong for this young preacher boy," Dad said.

I offered to help. "I'll cut up the *pulla*." Mom, like all other Finnish women, baked this sweet bread and served it to visitors with a cup of strong coffee. Soon, the sound of gurgling reached my ears. I stepped over to the stove as the water shot upward through the metal tube, then descended downwards after the water filled the basket to mix with the grounds. As the aroma of fresh brew filled the kitchen, I asked, "Do you use cream and sugar?"

"No. I drink it black." *Make a note of that.*

We'd visited with my parents for a while when Hilla showed up. Two years younger than me, she was the sister I shared a room with. A good kid, she probably followed the rules. Since living away from home, I knew little about her other than she had a boyfriend. Our elementary school teachers guided her to attend the academic elite high school, while I went into the commercial program at the composite high school. Hilla's dark wavy hair made her look like a movie star, her pointed nose and high cheekbones like our mother's. I just wished we had a closer connection. Her deep dimples when she smiled brought me tinges of jealousy.

"Hi. This is Antti. My pen pal from Finland." I turned to Antti and continued. "Hilla is in nursing school and is soon to graduate. She's way smarter than me."

Hilla walked to him and extended her hand for a courteous handshake. "I'm happy to meet you. I've seen so many letters come to our mailbox. And Pirkko's always reading letters or writing them and kicking me out of the room."

"Oh. Nice to meet you, too. She wrote a little about you. It's been quite a journey, writing and attending classes, and working with the churches. I've certainly been busy," Antti explained.

"Nursing school is very hard, and I feel like quitting sometimes."

Why didn't she tell me that? I wished we would talk more. But I lived out of town and she worked and attended college in our hometown.

Dad slurped his coffee and ate his sweet bread and moved to the living room. We'd chatted a while with Mom and Hilla when my cute little brother appeared. He could be a pest to older sisters, who wanted to keep adult talk away from his ears. Antti greeted him with a smile and asked him his age and teased him until they both laughed.

If walls revealed secrets, would Antti continue with me as our family issues were more than the average Christian family's, at least the ones in our circle? I compared our families, although his lived in Finland and he had divulged very little. His two sisters and two brothers probably lived in peace with their parents.

It was a pleasant visit, and we proved likable. Dad remained on his best behavior, not too rude. And Mom presented her normal quiet loving side and even joined us at the table for conversation. She, too, enjoyed the company. But where was my sister Laura, the subject of my letters? I should have asked Mom.

13

my youth group

A WEEK LATER, our youth group visited a church member's farm about thirty minutes from town. This time we drove in my brother Osmo's old Oldsmobile. All eight of us piled into the clunker and hoped it would make it to the destination. My seventeen-year-old brother took the driver's seat, and I hopped in beside him on the bench seat. Antti, slipped into the passenger side, placing me in the middle, and I tried to keep myself from touching him. Five other rowdy teenagers piled on top of each other in the back. The teasing began and lasted all the way to our destination. We weren't even dating, just friends meeting for the first time after two years of letter writing. We kept unwritten words between the lines in our hearts.

The young couple who owned the farm were recent immigrants to Canada. They also attended English language school but preferred to speak in Finnish. I visited them often at their house, as he was the brother of a youth leader and the pastor who just resigned. Many of our youth meetings took place out there in the countryside.

We all hopped onto the grassy field and slammed the car doors.

"Did I ever tell you about the time I talked about Zacchaeus to the youth?" I asked Antti and laughed.

Antti grasped his Bible in one hand as he stepped closer. "No. You never told me. I didn't know you preached."

"Well, I'm not a preacher, but sometimes I have the gift of a story that just comes out. You're like Zacchaeus, determined and eager to see your goal accomplished. You would do extraordinary things to get to a goal."

Antti pointed to the house as we walked toward where the others gathered in the yard. "Is the meeting inside or outside?" he asked and looked up to the sky. "It's getting cloudy. It might rain."

Clever. He changed the subject. A humble man as well. "Yes, I think we will meet inside. The bugs and blackflies are bad this time of year. But back to Zacchaeus, and the lesson the story brings us. Seek Jesus with all your heart and you will find him. That's what you've written about."

"True."

We ended our talk as we approached the group, and he took the joking directed at us in stride. Markus already strummed a guitar, indicating we'd soon start the service.

As someone so passionate about Jesus, I saw Antti as a good person who would do nothing wrong. Would he ever cheat on his taxes, like Zacchaeus? No, of course not. I believed him to be a man of integrity and even put him on a pedestal. An honorable man. I looked up to him.

After the meeting, we talked with Sofia while the others played games.

"What are your plans for next week?" Sofia asked.

"Do you mean me or Antti or both of us?"

"Both. Do you want to come over for supper one night? I'll make some Finnish meatballs and mashed potatoes. It's Antti's favorite."

I looked at Antti to answer, since his schedule with school and a church kept him busy. Our small congregation scheduled regular meetings during the week. On Thursday they held Bible Study, Saturday a prayer meeting, and Sunday included services both morning and evening. And as a serious student of the Scriptures and now English classes, Antti's schedule left little room for social time. I held my breath as I leaned closer. We sat on separate large boulders close to the driveway and darkness hid his face.

Finally, Antti turned toward Sofia and asked, "Yes. Would Tuesday work for you?"

Little flutters jumped in my belly. I hoped to see him alone, but I would take this any day. Osmo walked over and announced we would be leaving.

Once again, we said our goodbyes to the hosts and piled into the vehicle. A pleasant evening of singing songs and listening to Antti preach.

Trusting God as my source of joy filled my heart as I considered God's goodness and this moment. Driving on a dark country road, sitting beside a man of God's own heart, brought an unexplained happiness beyond words. Yet a sense of unworthiness lay like a wet blanket over my soul.

14

declaration of dating

WERE WE A couple or not? We made no official declaration of our dating status, not even to ourselves, but definitely not to others who, by now, counted us as a couple. One evening, during the first week after the conference, I invited Antti for a car ride in my father's black Chevy Impala. I didn't think much about it except I wanted to show him the sights of Thunder Bay, just as he'd shown me Lahti, Finland, his hometown, where we first met briefly at the crusade tent.

Now, two years later in Thunder Bay, he reminded me of the incident when he made the infamous announcement over the loudspeaker. "It was you!" Those words represented his initial thoughts of me, while I envisioned him taller. I imagined he probably felt a little perturbed by my comment about the big tent, but he never mentioned it again.

Antti's single-mindedness guided many of his actions, even when he would start dating, unknown to me. My pulse beat faster each time I saw him at the church services. Though we were friends through correspondence, I could not understand why he didn't ask me out. I'd never had a boyfriend but went on outings or dates with a few guys occasionally. But I never experienced anything like this, with such a strong attraction. To me, he was not like anyone else. His goal-oriented living mystified me. Passionate about God and the ministry, he had disclosed he wanted a wife someday to work alongside as a partner.

Our relationship was not like everyone else's. He pursued full-time ministry wholeheartedly, and I hovered between indecision about my future. I liked him. A lot. But I wasn't secure about his feelings and what he thought. Both of us must have felt we needed to be sure beyond any doubt before we announced it. I contemplated his testimony so many times and how it differed from mine. Our friendship was such a beautiful thing that I didn't want to mess it up.

Unlike Antti, I didn't have serious goals and dreams as a teenager so we were in different stages of life. When God called him to ministry as a teenager, there were no specifics about it, but he knew his goal. He grew up in a loving Christian family of five children with a mother and father and lived in a small farming village in Finland with relatives nearby, an ideal upbringing. They held many revival meetings, and over half the people of the town were Christians or believed in God. He attended a one-room country school with his siblings, cousins, and friends. Almost seventy percent of the students were Christian or from Christian homes. His parents also introduced the kids to visiting preachers, as many stayed at their home. Some relatives became preachers or supporters of ministries.

By age twenty-two, Antti had lived in Sweden for two years, running from the call of God, but grace spared his life until he surrendered. He dated a girl from the same church in Lahti, and by the time he entered Bible college in late August of 1968, they had dated for about a year.

Throughout the first few weeks of school, he wrestled with thoughts of selling out to God and if letting go of his girlfriend was the right thing. The hardest thing was to break off the relationship. Though he deeply cared for her and she liked him a lot, Antti didn't love her like he should love a woman. Then he found enough courage to break it off. His sensitive spirit didn't want to hurt her, but he knew there was no other way or they both would be in trouble. Not a simple thing to do, especially when he realized she didn't want to end it.

Growing up with two brothers close in age, Antti was the sibling who cared and waited for his two little sisters whenever they played in the fields or at the nearby lake. And while his brothers took off running, he walked home with the girls and held their hand if they got hurt.

After a few months at the seminary, his ex-girlfriend surprised him with a visit. She may have pretended to have come to see his sister, who worked as a cook in the school kitchen, but he sensed she wanted to reconcile. Before she left, however, they took a short walk and talked things over and parted on good terms. Though he was glad it was over, it still pained him to see her so sad. For years, Antti couldn't get over the fact that he'd hurt her by breaking off the relationship. As a principled man, Antti made a declaration to himself and to God.

When he revealed this to me, it took me by surprise. He wouldn't date until the right one came along and his heart revealed she would be the one to marry. Then he added, as an afterthought, he wouldn't date until his last year of seminary. He had shared this with friends and classmates whenever they would tease him or try to act as a matchmaker.

"Are you sure?" They couldn't believe his resolve.

After he told me this, it explained his reservations about announcing our dating relationship. He wanted to be sure. I understood that clearly. We had long conversations about this.

I dropped my hands on my lap as I listened to his story about his past girlfriend. Now it made so much more sense why I couldn't read him.

"It was the hardest thing for me to not date anyone for three and a half years. There were so many pretty girls at the college and at church, but somehow God spared me and wouldn't allow me to connect with a girl."

"Wow, that's incredible. But how did it work out? You didn't ask anyone out?" I could hardly believe it, but I knew he was a man of integrity so he wouldn't lie.

"No, I prayed. 'God help me. I'm yours.'"

"I can see how your friends would think how stupid you were."

"But I had to live up to that promise no matter how hard it was."

"Now I understand why you're so careful," I said. "And yes, we both need to be sure."

Antti's final year would begin in a few weeks so he'd be free to date again. And that's why it took so long for us to come up with the official decision.

In the years after their breakup, Antti had dug deeper into his soul and realized his own pain caused him to make such a difficult declaration. He had hurt a girl once and would not do it ever again. He finally understood he carried someone else's offense. Each person must carry his or her own hurts and forgive oneself as well as the other person. Relationships can't always work out and as long as you do the right thing, you have no reason to carry any guilt. Eventually, his ex-girlfriend moved on with her life and married someone else.

AFTER THE BIBLE Study on Thursday night, I walked up to Antti in the lobby and asked, "Would you like to go on a hike next Saturday?" I wanted to spend time alone with him to clarify his feelings about us.

"Where?"

"Up the famous Mount McKay. It's a unique landmark in the area, on the Native Reservation. I'll tell you about it later."

"How long will it take?"

"We could make it in a couple of hours. It's not too far from here."

Mount McKay stood 1,585 feet above sea level on the south side of town on the Fort William First Nation Reserve. We could see it from Hillcrest Park, in the north part of the city, where I lived.

I harbored a secret motive as well. Private time with Antti with no distractions from others. Family. Friends. Church people. Even strangers in cafes or stores wanted to strike up a conversation about Finland.

Since Saturday was the only suitable day of the week, we decided on it because Antti attended English classes Monday to Friday and I worked full-time for the government. He kept Sundays to himself and the congregation to visit with people.

After a long pause, he said, "That would be nice. What time do you want to go?"

"How about ten o'clock?" I suggested.

Antti waved to a couple with a funny smirk on their faces as they walked out of the church building. "That's good. It gives enough time for me to get ready for Sunday."

A lunch of rye bread with ham and a thermos of coffee should give us energy for the day. Cinnamon buns would add a sugar rush as well. And we would be back before supper.

I drove to Antti's hosts' home on Empress Avenue in my father's black Chevy, hoping to have enough gas. My sister also used the vehicle, and each of us added just enough for our own needs, but often the gauge showed empty. Sometimes, though, Dad would leave it full and then expected us to pay our own way. Of course, after Friday night, the Chevy needed gas, which I used as an excuse for why I was late.

Once we drove through the neighborhood streets, Antti asked, "How long will it take to get there?"

If I didn't hit any curbs or get a flat tire, or run out of gas, it wouldn't take too long. But I didn't tell him that. "Twenty or thirty minutes at the most. I think I remember the direction, the shortest way." Our youth group hiked the trails there a few years ago.

Antti remained silent while I drove and focused on the road. The drive to the south side of town from the north took us through several city streets and across a CN Rail metal drawbridge that crossed the Kaministiquia River. It was nothing pretty to look at, but we had to cross it to get to the native reserve lands where the road to the mountain began. Compared to the Alps or the Rockies, people would consider Mount McKay a small hill, but to us locals, it was a humongous mountain.

I concentrated on driving the narrow gravel road while Antti silently looked ahead. *Is he apprehensive about my driving?* The road wound around curves and ascended for what seemed like forever. I drove in the middle, as the drop on the passenger side was steep. Luckily, no other vehicles came toward us.

After we paid the small entrance fee to the parking area, we got out and stood near the edge to view the sights. The breathtaking view from this level seemed enough to take in and stay awhile. But we were only halfway up the mountain. We needed to get to the top to enjoy nature and the views of the city and surrounding area. From this vantage point, the Kaministiquia River meandered around flat terrain near its mouth at Lake Superior and divided into two tributaries. You could almost distinguish businesses. The airport was easy to spot as well as the grain elevators.

I snuck in glances at Antti's profile while he drank in the scenery. What a lucky girl I was to be with him! Alone at last. Would there be more to discover about him? His feet were beautiful, though I couldn't see them through his runners. Scriptures say that the feet of those who bring the good news of the gospel are beautiful. So much to talk about, and this was our chance. *What else is there to know about the man I'm trudging up a treacherous path on mountainous terrain with?* Would there be a future with him? Or would he return to his homeland after a summer of ministry, terminating our correspondence? *You're overthinking this. Just enjoy the moment.*

Finally, after a long silence, I asked, "What are you thinking about?"

"How beautiful God's earth is with the mountains and valleys. Looks like this part of the city is flat. I see some hills farther away. Is that where the church is?" Antti pointed toward the distance.

"Yes. We live on the north side, which used to be called Port Arthur, and this part was called Fort William. They amalgamated two years ago, and there's been rivalry ever since."

"Oh, there must be a reason." Antti's eyes widened as if in disbelief. I didn't explain further, as we had to get going.

We walked around the area for a while and found a private spot for a picnic. Nature flourished in July. Greenery, wildflowers, and shrubs burst with life everywhere. Long grass. The sounds of birds and crickets. Pines trees and some birch provided shade from the noon sun.

After we ate our lunch, I said, "I think we should hike to the top, where the view is phenomenal." We strolled around some grassy areas. "It's not too far. I was there with our youth group a few years ago. It's so much better than here, and we're halfway already."

My friends had teased us about the trails and the hike, and how we could get lost easily. I assured them it wasn't that hard. Antti seemed to like the idea. "How long do you think it will take to get to the top?" He tilted his head and shielded his eyes from the sun, and looked up at the rocky part of the mountain. It frightened me to stare at the steep cliff in front of us. Only rock climbers with proper equipment would make it alive.

I assured him there were original trails on the other side, and we wouldn't need to try anything too difficult. "About thirty minutes. Depends on how fast we go."

"Do you know the way? Are there trails already marked?"

"Yes, many tourists and hikers use the trails. I think there are even ropes to hold in the steep parts. If I can do it, you won't have any problems." I sized him up as athletic and physically fit, even though he'd been in school all year. He jogged, biked, and played volleyball.

I pointed toward some bushy shrubbery. "Okay, let's go. I think the trail starts over there." While searching for the exact starting point, my skin flushed with the heat of the morning, but we soon arrived at a slight opening in the deep underbrush. "There."

My heart rejoiced as we started the climb. We would soon enjoy the magnificent view, but that wasn't really the reason for my joy. I wanted to spend time with him sitting on top of the mountain, both literally and figuratively. Explore each other's intentions. Or just make conversation. Letters didn't provide such an avenue properly. So many misunderstandings while waiting weeks for an answer to a simple question. Where would our lives take us? Two long years of correspondence as complete strangers. The original plan of English lessons fell by the wayside early on. He gave the excuse he was too busy with schoolwork and didn't want to extend his brain for English lessons, so he wrote mostly in Finnish. I was fine with that.

The steep climb and rugged trail proved to be harder than I remembered. Steady incline. At one point, I slipped backward as I stepped on loose shale. Antti caught me from behind and held my hand until I stabilized. I suggested he go first. I didn't want to stumble in front of him again, revealing my clumsiness or backside.

Soon we stumbled to a flat, grassy ground where we rested before trudging toward the edge of the cliffs. So glad we made it without too many mishaps. I wanted to take advantage of every opportunity of our time together. I warmed up to him and my cheeks blushed, but I desired his undivided attention. "Let's sit here." I pointed to a large, flat boulder. "I should have brought a blanket."

After we found a comfortable spot, Antti pulled out his backpack. "It's okay, we don't need a blanket. Let's eat the rest of the lunch."

I watched him and said, "One sandwich left. You can have it. I'm not hungry." I took the bottle of juice he offered and shook the thermos to see if any coffee remained. "Some left. Do you want any?"

"No. I'm okay. You have it." After hours of conversation and enjoying the view, we looked at each other and the disappearing sun. I pulled on my light jacket. Neither of us noticed the blackflies swarming around. Suddenly, Antti slapped his forearm to kill a little bug. I laughed as blood splashed on his skin. "Have you read the blackflies suck blood from you and leave a hole the size of a dime?"

The wind died down, and the sun already moved farther to the west, behind some trees.

"Really? I doubt that. We have mosquitos in Finland, and I've never heard of this."

"No, these are not flies or mosquitos, but blackflies, smaller. They are nasty bloodsuckers. That's the negative side of living in Northwestern Ontario. They come out in June and July, during the warmest part of the summer, usually in the evening."

Antti glanced at me with skepticism. "We better get going, as the sun will soon be far behind the forest, and the trails will be hard to see."

With a little thump, we both dropped to solid ground from the large boulder. "Okay. Yes. Let's go." I searched for the trail. "I can't remember where the trail starts downward. I didn't pay attention when we were here with the youth group. The leaders led the way. I hope we can find it."

Antti showed no expression, but, secretly, I suddenly feared the worst. What if it grew dark before we get to the parking lot? We didn't even have a flashlight.

After what seemed like hours, although probably only minutes, we found an opening in the thick underbrush that looked like a trail. We began our descent. I led the way this time. We needed to get out of there before dark, or we'd never find our way. The dirt path meandered, slightly ascending and then descending the steep slope. When I stopped to consider the next step, Antti took my hand. Little butterflies fluttered in my stomach. How nice to feel his touch. Comforting. Being near him pushed away worry and anxiety. The trail widened and leveled, so we held hands as we walked. A leisurely stroll as we talked about our meeting for the first time, and our brief interaction two years ago in Finland. Lost in conversation, dark skies and the cool air overtook us. The forest seemed to howl with eerie sounds. Where was the sun? Behind the mountain now, leaving only a slight glow through the trees that faintly lit the path.

During our slow descent, the pathway separated from the main one. Suddenly, I forgot which way we climbed up the steep rocky trail. "Do you remember if we came up this way?" I asked Antti with panic pounding in my ears. *I can't tell him we're lost. He'll think I'm a basket case.* I sensed he had expert direction from his comments about the sun. I usually paid no attention to the setting sun or its direction.

"No. But the sun is slipping away fast. Soon it will be total darkness. Why don't we pray and ask God to help us?" Antti suggested.

"Sure. But we need to decide if we go back to the fork in the trail or keep going this way." I lifted my hands in the air with exasperation.

Just as the sun descended behind the other side of the mountain and darkness covered the land, we arrived in the grassy area near the parking lot. As if on cue, we whispered,

"Thank God." We locked arms together and trudged toward a dark shadow, the Chevy, the only vehicle in the parking lot.

What did I learn? That I needed to pay attention to the position of the sun. And to trust God and His care for us. That I remain securely anchored on the Rock of our salvation. "I lift my eyes to the mountains—where does my help come from?" We found our way back.

The beginning of a beautiful dating relationship brewed as we looked to the Lord in prayer. My feelings intensified after this experience. I came to trust a man for the first time. We moved to a more-than-friends status. More than pen pals to a dating couple.

15

sprouting seeds of love

WE HAD PROGRESSED to something more. Our time together allowed us to get to know one another and for me to realize I held deeper emotions than physical attraction. Our mountain adventure foreshadowed subsequent climbs our relationship would endure. Would the long distance, especially across the vast ocean, survive the longing of the heart? As the climb tested my trust in God and in a man, I wondered about the future. Happy the next day was Sunday and I would meet him again, it didn't matter that his focus was on his sermon or "pastoring" the people of the church; I craved a portion of his day. We were officially a couple, at least that's what I understood, although we didn't clarify it verbally. I would sit in the pew at every opportunity. And he, at the pulpit looking over the congregation, avoided looking at me. His manner of focus. *Would I become a distraction for him?*

As our few precious moments together passed like a freight train steady on its tracks, our time would soon end. Since the clock ticked to its inevitable outcome, we spent every evening together and just talked and talked. The meaningful discussions became a lifeline for our destinies, nothing like I'd ever experienced before. I thought about Antti during the day and waited for the evening when we would see each other. Sometimes I used my father's vehicle, and other times my brother allowed Antti to drive his Oldsmobile, the floating boat-like vehicle. When Antti drove it, I shimmied to the middle of the wide seat to be near him. The warmth of his body next to mine gave me a cozy, secure feeling.

The fuzzy feelings continued every time we were together, and even in his absence, my heart throbbed for this young seminary student and visiting minister. How did this happen? Who can tame the heart? Would we kiss sometime? Two weeks passed by, and we enjoyed each other's company and the friendship it provided. One evening when I drove Antti back to the home where he stayed, I parked the car on the street in front of the house and cut the engine for our usual talk and prayer. He shifted closer and placed his arms around my shoulders. We talked into the wee hours of the morning, finally forced to acknowledge it was time to part, but not before a tender moment for the first kiss. With our gaze on each other, I inhaled his presence and lingered, waiting for the kiss. Then our lips touched for the first time. After the kiss, we hugged, and I rested my head on his chest. Then he said the words I'd been longing to hear. "I love you."

I replied, "I love you too."

On the drive home, I could hardly focus on the road, mesmerized by the taste of his lips and the softness of his embrace. So pure and beautiful.

The last week before his departure, we took a road trip to a town where our family lived when I was thirteen and fourteen. Another opportunity to spend quality time together while visiting a place where I lived as a young teen. The four-hour drive to Nakina would be perfect for those conversations we had put off. The hard ones. Of what I had been like as a young teenager. Would I go there?

We would have to be oblivious to the teasing or gossip that would come on our return, but we didn't care. It was our choice. In those days, Christian dating couples seldom slept together. What were we doing?

At this point in our relationship, we probably should have those talks that counselors suggest pre-marriage. What dreams did we have for our future in regard to children, money, sex, and communication? But none of those came to mind, as we hadn't even talked about marriage. We had bigger issues to deal with, like the stormy ocean between us. We left Thunder Bay in anticipation and yet with trepidation on my part.

We arrived in Nakina on Friday night while it was still light out and drove past the old house where we lived the two years while my dad worked as a lumberjack at Kimberly Clark, a large paper mill. The two-story building with grayish peeling paint remained there, dilapidated. I had claimed the upstairs to myself, where I read Nancy Drew books and others. No one else wanted it since it had no heat.

Though my parents didn't speak enough English to understand the preaching, our family attended the local Pentecostal church. Dad believed children should be in Sunday school, and my parents enjoyed the spiritual atmosphere. The friendly pastors took us in with loving arms as part of the church family.

As we cruised around town, an old jalopy of a car parked on a gravel road triggered a memory. Suddenly I stopped talking. *Should I share the experience or not?* A girlfriend and I had met up with some teenage boys, old enough to have a license and a car. Something like a double date. We had traveled around town, and they drove us home. She lived next door, so they parked between the two houses on the opposite side of the street, near a dim light pole.

We parked at my old school lot, and I turned to Antti. "Do you know what?"

He looked at me. A slight line creased his forehead. "No. What else is there to see around town?"

I hesitated with my head toward the passenger window. "Nothing much, as you can see. But I have something to tell you. From my past." Heat welled up my neck to my face. At least dusk had settled, and he couldn't make out the redness crawling up my cheek. I had never told this story to anyone.

"Okay. Here goes. You can laugh or think how stupid I was." My eyes dropped to my hands as I fiddled with my purse on my lap and recalled the humiliating story about being in the back seat of a car with a hormonal teenage boy. "When the boy pushed closer than I was comfortable with, I pried the door open and burst out."

After what seemed like an eternity, Antti acknowledged my feelings. "I'm sure it scared you, but you got out. You don't have to be afraid of what I'm thinking. You were fourteen."

"But it was dumb of me. I should have known better."

Antti lifted his arm across my shoulders and pulled me closer and whispered, "I'm glad you told me that story. Makes me love you more."

"Thanks. I'm so glad. It was difficult, and I was afraid you wouldn't love me." I rested my head on his shoulder and breathed a sigh of relief. "I think we should head back to the pastor's house. They're probably wondering where we are."

"Yes. Let's get going." Antti turned the ignition and drove the few blocks.

We arrived at the manse and planned to do more exploring the next day, Saturday. The pastor and his wife welcomed us with open arms to their small apartment at the back of the church building. I had been there many times for youth meetings and just to hang out. They were wonderful people who loved to entertain and made us feel at home. They even understood Antti's strong Finnish accent because they had met several Finnish families with broken English.

After some banter and serious discussion, we needed to get some sleep. With trepidation, I asked, "Where are we going to sleep?" I wasn't sure if they had separate bedrooms for us or not.

They had already taken care of that problem and pointed to the sleeping area. The pastor's wife opened one door and said, "Pirkko, you sleep here in our guest room." Then she turned to Antti and walked to the other side of the hallway. "Our son was excited to give you his bedroom for the night. He's okay on the couch."

"Thank you," I said.

The Lord had already ordered our steps, even about the bedrooms. We had not yet discussed sleeping together before marriage, but we didn't need to. Our similar upbringing served its purpose.

Though our lives intertwined physically, emotionally, and spiritually during this summer, I had never planned on dating a pastor or a missionary. Could love be blind? Or was I playing with his heart and mine? A declaration I made to myself as a foolish teenager now played in my mind. Not to marry a pastor or someone like my father. Our dating relationship was in its infancy, and we both were acutely aware our time would end soon. We didn't know if there was a tomorrow for us with the many insurmountable obstacles in the way. Our career choices, cultural differences, and the physical distance between us. Transatlantic flights would be an enormous economic hardship, and phone calls were too expensive. Where would his ministry take him after graduation next summer? It didn't seem likely he would be back in Canada. And I had three more years of university. And the denomination would require a commitment to a pastorship before they would ever consider him as a mission's candidate.

If the mountain of doubt were removed and cast into the sea, and seeds of love sprouted through the obstacles, it would be worth it. Faith and patience would grow during the wait. God promises perfect love casts out all fear if we put our trust in Him. Is there anything too hard for God?

16

end of summer

IF THERE WAS a fairytale ending, ours would not be it. Not
at that time, at least. Throughout the last six weeks of summer,
I transitioned from calculated aloofness to something I couldn't
even admit to myself. If I'd considered the complexity of the
consequences of our relationship, I would have ended it before
it broke my heart into a thousand pieces. Never having been in
love, this was unfamiliar territory. But I had vowed to myself at
the beginning of the summer, when we met, that if Antti didn't
make a move toward me, then I wouldn't pursue love and
would happily remain single for the rest of my life.

Before the summer ended, I probed deep into my soul,
fearing this would not last. My brain warned that he was out of

reach for me for the long term. Not in my league regarding God's calling, as I believed that if God calls the man or woman, then he would call the partner as well. Throughout our correspondence, Antti's love for God and the work of the ministry shone so brightly that it might have blinded me.

Time had been too short for an intimate relationship to develop, but our physical attraction kept us together, and our developing spiritual unity kept us grounded. We shared our hopes and dreams. And the oddity of our relationship kept us leaning on God for help to endure the upcoming separation that would test our commitment.

Though my feelings for Antti deepened with every passing day, I often felt as if I wasn't enough or up to his spiritual standards. He prayed and read his Bible regularly. My devotional life sputtered like a gas lawnmower in the summer rain. Sometimes it would start and other times it didn't. He had written about the importance of consistent devotions, which I made promises to myself about, but then broke all too often. I didn't measure up as a Christian or as someone who dated a pastoral candidate.

Before my boyfriend left at the end of the summer, my mind flowed with questions. Would he ever come back? Would we meet again? What did he really think about my family?

Though we both grew up in a traditional Christian family, we were different. His was close, and ours more distant. And his loving siblings certainly caused no troubles like ours, a comparison that held me hostage for a while, and that made little sense since I'd never even met his parents, nor his siblings. But what he expressed in his letters about his home life and his relationship with his parents and brothers and sisters made me somewhat jealous. We'd suffered the negative effects of immigration to a new country, such as poverty and language barriers, while they had only moved upwards—from a modest farm to the city in Finland. We lived in a small bungalow with a messy yard on the poor side of town, and they lived in a large two-story corner house in a pleasant neighborhood with manicured lawns.

On one of our dates, we stopped in the parking lot at Hillcrest Park, but since it was still daylight, we strolled around the park to the sunken garden area, in its magnificent bloom, to enjoy each other's company in the shadow of brilliant flowers.

We needed to get acquainted at a deeper level from pen and paper so we conversed, often into early morning hours, and laughed at the strenuous circumstances of our lives. Nothing seemed normal to us as a dating couple like other young people experienced during high school or college. No love at first sight, but a deeper, slower growth, beginning with spiritual intimacy and quickly bonding emotionally. Antti's love for prayer directed our dating, as we usually prayed before ending an evening.

After we sat on the bench in the middle of the garden for a time, the sun slipped behind the trees and the air cooled. So, we wandered back to the car arm in arm. We drove off to my place, down the hill from the park where I housesat for my employers where we had total privacy. There on the couch, we snuggled and talked for another hour until it was time to go. His soft kiss on the lips anchored our relationship physically as well as emotionally. Suddenly, I wanted to share my heart, or at least open it a bit before the clock struck midnight. He would leave on Tuesday morning, and tomorrow would be his last evening with our family so tonight was the last night we'd have alone time together before separating for the unknown future. I thanked God for how He'd orchestrated our lives so far, even when I resisted and fought against His plan.

I moved away and turned to face him, crossing my arms over my chest. "I waited for you to ask me out the first week, but you didn't. That disappointed me. I sat in the services the whole weekend dreaming you would broach the subject."

He stared down at his hands and placed one hand on my knee. "I know. I'm sorry. I didn't really want to date until I was sure."

"I wondered about that. Why you were so hesitant, but I kind of analyzed it in my head," I replied.

After a few minutes, his eyes narrowed. "How? I couldn't discern what you were thinking."

I answered as honestly as I could. "That you're too single-minded and only thought about the ministry at the church. And only cared about me as a friend, like we'd been since we'd corresponded for two years. I'm sorry for not always replying to your letters consistently, but at least we got acquainted with each other."

"Oh. I agree I'm principled, but I also didn't think it was a good idea to drive alone in your car if we weren't a dating couple."

"It doesn't matter what people think. Or if they judge us. And strangers wouldn't even wonder about it."

"I am old-fashioned that way."

"Yes, you are." I got up off the couch, but Antti pulled me back for another hug.

With his arms around my waist, he added, "But now we're a couple, and I'm overjoyed how our love has blossomed so sweetly. Beautiful."

"And to think I had planned to spend the summer in Mexico! I wasn't too keen on you coming to Thunder Bay. My thoughts remain a mystery."

Antti's wide smile conveyed it all. "I'm happy you stayed."

We hugged again while my heart expanded. I didn't want to lose something so beautiful. Would we see each other again? The old couch caught us in a cozy place where I could stay with him for a long time. Antti rose first and pulled me up, and we walked to the porch area with his arms wrapped around my waist. But before I picked up my keys to drive him back to his hosts' house, he stepped closer, and we embraced. We connected emotionally and joyful tears wet my eyes. How could this have happened to me when I didn't deserve it? I could totally trust this man and submit to his loving touch with no fear. I loved him so much. And he loved me. He would treat me with respect.

Thoughts of uncertainty continued to float in my brain. Would this be the last time we cuddled? Would he come back? This couldn't be happening like this. He was leaving. What if he found someone else? If I wasn't good enough, then there was no use continuing. *Maybe stop writing letters.* The future remained totally uncertain. His life's trajectory seemed so certain, at least the ministry part, and mine confusing and uncertain. I still searched for purpose. Could I suit as a pastor's wife? Or as a missionary's partner?

Why would Antti choose me above all the cute girls in Finland? Many studied at the same seminary. We had a mutual female friend with whom I corresponded. Antti's choices were plentiful, but would he waver on his commitment if I messed this relationship up with my confusion about God's guidance?

On Monday I worked while Antti packed and visited with church people. Time seemed to drag on at a snail's pace, but the girls in the office kept me entertained and teased me until my face turned red. No, we had done nothing they accused me of. They didn't know my boyfriend like I did.

The minutes stretched on and on as I tapped my pencil on the desk. The girls next to me smiled. *I've been pretty useless today.* I peeked at my watch every few minutes. Wasn't it time yet? Four-thirty couldn't have come soon enough. Finally, I pulled my purse from under the drawer and headed toward the elevator. "See you tomorrow," I told the staff who, by now, were used to my anxious behavior.

Stopping nowhere, I drove straight to the Rantas house and picked him up. My parents invited Antti for a last supper, so we drove there. Dad greeted us at the door while Mom hustled in the kitchen, and my younger siblings hung around giggling.

"It's so good to visit your parents one last time," Antti assured me as we walked in. Though we had not spent a lot of time at my home, he had become comfortable with my father. Both my parents liked my boyfriend and enjoyed his company, as did the church people.

My father and boyfriend had one fundamental quality in common. Otherwise, they were as different as the ocean and the lake. One like a stormy sea, and the other like glassy waters reflecting the sky and clouds. But they were both passionate for souls and the church ministry. I had declared only a few years prior that I would not marry someone like my father, but that summer my beliefs transformed. I loved my boyfriend more than anyone in the world and placed him on a pedestal.

I saw my father with fresh eyes. Medium built with a full head of wavy thick dark hair with a straight nose, he was pretty good-looking. He was courageous, bold, and strong as he had brought our family to Canada to provide a better life. My father lacked formal education but taught himself to study the Bible and became somewhat of a successful preacher through his insightful expounding of the Scriptures. He inspired his listeners with his funny stories and displayed uncanny humor in all seriousness. Sometimes we couldn't decipher if the message was funny or serious. He worked as a farm laborer and an independent contractor in the forest industry, felling trees and transporting logs to paper mills. Though he lacked some cultural awareness and lived his life on his own terms, he instilled the value of hard work in his kids and lived with passion for the things of God.

In his later years, we joked about his memory. He never forgot his Bible. He placed them all over, wherever he spent time regularly. One stayed by his bedside table at the wilderness bunker where men worked and slept for weeks on end. He wasn't afraid to defend his beliefs to the rough crowd, even when they made fun of him. Another place that a Bible remained was in his pew at church. He didn't take it home because he had Bibles in every room, it seemed. The dashboard of his truck always had one or two. An extra one for giving away.

"I wish we had more time," I said. All I desired was to be alone with Antti and to downplay the significance my father would play in our future lives.

Mom set the table, but the meal was not quite ready, so Antti visited with Dad in the living room. I helped with the finishing touches, like cutting rye bread and adding napkins, which we rarely used.

Soon, Mom called from the kitchen, "Supper is ready." My mother, a petite woman, picked up the large pot of steaming potatoes and placed it on a potholder on the table. She had grown up on a large farm in Finland and was used to hard physical labor. Every summer, Mom dug and tilled the soil in our small backyard to grow root vegetables such as potatoes and carrots.

When the meal of potatoes, gravy, and meat waited on the oval kitchen table, we all sat down and Antti asked to say a prayer. He thanked God for the time he had spent with our family and the church, with a special emphasis on blessing the food and our future life together.

"When you return to Thunder Bay, I'll fix you fried fish," Dad said. He also added jokingly, "And I'll even come to visit you in Ecuador to cook it for you." My father often spoke prophetically and directly about issues.

"Antti, Dad likes his fish and loves fishing, but funnily, I can't eat it. Every time he fries fish, I itch, so I have to leave the house or go in my room and close the door."

Antti, being a gentleman, smiled and accepted his offer graciously. "That would be nice. Not sure about Ecuador yet."

After the meal, I helped Mom clean up and commanded my sister to wash the dishes so we could leave. I just wanted to be alone with my boyfriend. He said his goodbyes to everyone and playfully acknowledged my young sister and brother by reassuring them he would see them again. Everyone remained on their best behavior, and we had a great time.

Antti hugged my mother, who laughed nervously, not knowing what to do. Our family wasn't the touchy feely type and didn't often display physical affection. "Thank you for the delicious meal. I have to say goodbye and hope to see you again someday." Mom tapped him on the arm and turned around to attend to her chores.

Dad stuck his hand out for a firm handshake and said, "You're welcome back anytime. Maybe I'll even come to preach in Finland."

It saddened me to realize one person was missing. *Where is she?*

17

come back to me

AFTER ANTTI LEFT, exhaustion hit me, but I started a long letter that formed over three days. Between my fatigue and work, I just couldn't write it all in one day. When Antti phoned from Toronto before flying to Finland, my heart beat faster. We still had so much to talk about and hearing his voice lifted my spirits.

Thunder Bay
Tuesday, August 1, 1972

My Love,
This is my first evening without you. It's only nine o'clock and I'm so tired, but can't sleep. I worked all day and was almost late, but only for

five minutes. Amazingly, I could work. In the evening we had our family camp planning meeting where I was of no help, but when I came home a little after eight, it felt wistfully strange because there was nothing else. You were gone from here, and life seemed on pause, and I can't do anything. Though your place here is empty, you are in my heart every moment. I don't have words to describe my emotions at this moment, but I'm sure you can read my thoughts. Dear Antti, I didn't imagine how difficult it would be to separate from you. I pray the Lord will give me what I need in the days ahead so I feel secure. It hasn't even been a day since we separated with a hug, but already so much time has gone by. Time has passed and my eyes close and great tiredness overtakes me, so I'll drop into bed. I'll continue tomorrow.

Goodnight, love.

Wednesday, August 2, 1972

This evening before I left for church, I looked at your photo on the mirror and noticed a script on the back, To Pirkko 2/8/71 Antti. *That date is exactly a year ago to the day when you wrote those words. What thoughts did you have then? Though you did not know of happenings a year ahead, God gave patience for the right timing and kept us apart to mature us for each other. If you had dated through letters or if you came here sooner, perhaps it would not have worked out. I would not have been ready and would have only looked through rose-colored glasses elsewhere. Of course, walking in God's plan will happen as He's already ordered our steps, but as humans, we make it complicated by hurrying or slowing. How the Lord amazingly guides; we could not have planned it ourselves so well. God kept us separate for two years while we sought His will. It is so wonderful we began our courtship with prayer, blessing each other, and the same with our separation, knowing we won't see each other. Our last prayer time was so emotional. I prayed so earnestly. I did not understand the significance of it in that night hour, but now I think of all it entails. God's blessing surely was present. For years I've wanted to surrender all of my life to the Lord. I felt I couldn't give my whole life and always held on to something. It was so great to commit fully to God's work, knowing I won't be alone. God knows how much we can bear and how we can work in His ministry.*

Saturday, August 5, 1972

I'm alone at Sofia's place looking after her cats, as she traveled to Longlac. I read the magazines and sent inquiries to many schools. I also wrote to a friend in Toronto and told her about my fantastic summer experience. She seemed surprised. Then Pastor Murtonen's son phoned. We talked for half an hour. Then I went home and from there to their house because they invited me. Even though he was tired, he was happy. He liked his trip and said it was sad to leave. He had visited Santala with a friend. Oh my, now almost everyone has been there, and I only see it through other people's eyes. Santala has become familiar and precious to me. One day I will visit there.

The pastor's wife was especially interested in our budding romance. I shared with them how we greeted each other at the tent crusade two years ago and you didn't know who I was. I remember when I walked from the doorway to the front of the altar. You stood on the platform. "That was you!" You said something like that. At that moment, neither of us could have fathomed that the other would become their life partner. My only thought was that you were too short. Nothing more.

They are so happy for us. Told me to send you greetings. They always remember to encourage me now that I'm alone. The summer, as life-changing as it was, couldn't have gone any better. I didn't really plan to come to Thunder Bay because you would be there, and I wanted an adventure in Mexico. But our Heavenly Father had other plans. I love you because God led us together and you love Jesus and His work. At first, I feared your rigid stance on topics, but then I realized you weren't any more dogmatic than me. We are not the same. I never envisioned I would love a man who loves his work more than his wife, or in our case, girlfriend. I respected what you voiced at the Rantas' even before we started dating. I will try to remember to focus my love on my Savior as a priority and then on you.

I remember how you told me about your mission call to Ecuador when we met briefly in Jyvaskyla and that you had not revealed it to many people. Why did you tell me back then? You haven't mentioned it. I was a little shocked then but forgot about it. Perhaps unconsciously, I've connected my life to that knowledge in these past two years. Anyway, God knows everything and we can journey in His guided path.

I'm on my third pen already as ink blots to paper. Someone gave a penny for my pen collection, and I'll get paper from work. All I need are envelopes and stamps! Wow, what an exciting life! Oh, Antti dear, you are so far! Wonder how the winter will be? If the Lord has taken care of us so far, then why would He not take care when we are so far from each other? I miss you many times. Remembering you in my prayers.

Loving you always,
Your Pirkko

God had been good to us that summer. I anxiously waited for a letter and one finally arrived in my mailbox two weeks after he left. He had spent a few days in Toronto but made the phone call and wrote to me on the flight home.

Tuesday, August 8, 1972
Airplane 6:45 p.m.

Pirkko, My Love,
As I sat in the airport waiting area after getting my papers processed, melancholy set in, and I missed you. Like I had to let go of someone to whom I had become attached. The same feeling once again when the flight took off.

You were sweet because you weren't angry that I wasn't available when you phoned. It was nice to phone you back, as I liked how your voice

136

was so wonderfully sleepy. Although I've been busy, I have missed you so many times.

I keep thinking about you, Pirkko, my love. My heart feels funny in a way I can't explain. But I'm safe. We are together through letters and also through prayer.

I was glad to visit Niagara Falls. As I walked through Niagara Falls Park under the streetlights, I longed for you so much. It would have been beautiful to stroll with you alone. Everything looked so romantic.

God's finger has directed everything so far. The same in the future. Good to look ahead in peace knowing He has promised to guide us as we walk in prayer. Amen! I can't explain in words the emotions I have in my life about this. It's something that only Christian young people who have found each other can experience.

I've left now, Pirkko, but I didn't leave for eternity. I will return one day, and I want to own you forever. God's timetable is happening in our lives all continuously, while we don't see it or understand it.

I keep reminiscing about my time in Thunder Bay, especially our time together. It was something so beautiful, unlike anything I ever experienced.

Our heavenly Father has been so good, Pirkko. The entire summer was God's guidance for me in everything. Neither one of us know how many times we will have to separate before we can be together. You are so soft. I love you. (The only English words in this letter.)

I just ate at eight-thirty p.m. and now it's nine-thirty p.m. and I'm going to sleep. The sun set an hour ago, but now it's rising. The horizon is so beautiful. I can see Iceland's dark scenery. The night didn't come, only dusk. I'll try to sleep. Good night, my dear.

I will close my eyes and nod off with thoughts about you. I miss you and long for you and miss you.

Your Antti

Though his letter spoke of his love, I vacillated between the reality of long-distance love being true and trusting my heart. We found ourselves at a crossroads. Would our feelings sustain us through the unknown winter ahead while he finished his studies? Then what? If I followed through on my education, I would still have three more years. How would God put all this together? I understood Antti would be obligated to a pastorship through his denomination, at least for a few years, or he would have to pay the tuition back, but how? And where? I convinced myself that maybe we weren't able to last in a long-distance relationship for three more years. And as one called by God, Antti was totally focused on his purpose for ministry, and it would be impossible to separate him from that. So, what would he do? Should I continue our correspondence while pursuing my education? *And can I trust this will work out? God, help me!*

It surprised me that I fell so hopelessly in love so quickly. What if this was a summer fling that would fizzle out as time passed and we each went on with our lives? Was there any purpose in following this onerous path and navigating the tremendous obstacles that lay ahead? But for God's providence, there would be no future for us as a couple. Since I had never had my heart broken this way, I kept the worst scenarios in my mind so if anything happened, I wouldn't get hurt as badly.

We had climbed Mount McKay and almost lost our way in the descent. One day a few weeks after we separated, our mountain experience became a reminder of unattainable obstacles, but I consoled myself that nothing proved impossible for our God. Determined to keep focused on the direction we had embarked, allowing love to lead the way, my mind found peace through prayer.

Fortunately, my mind stilled in the face of this separation as I submitted to follow my heart and the love of my life. I trusted he did the same. But I still had not shared my deepest secret, which could sever our relationship. Was it worth it? Do dating couples need to share everything from the past with a potential future spouse? According to Scripture, which we tried to live by, there should be no secrets going into a marriage.

18

desperate for god

AFTER WE SEPARATED and peeked into the unknown
future, I kept myself busy the rest of the summer, all too aware
of my own shortcomings, including disappointment in
unanswered prayers. Antti's passion for God and the ministry
forced me to assess my own spiritual life. Would I ever be
strong enough for the life he represented in our conversations
during the summer?

I obligated myself to seek God intentionally, practically in
desperation. I had hung around Pentecostal young people for
years and watched many friends experience the filling of the
Holy Spirit. In my mind, it required consecration, dedication,
and holiness, but I felt unworthy. Though I attended church, I

lacked knowledge about spiritual gifts and how God's grace covers all our sins and weaknesses, and we don't earn salvation by works. All I needed was to submit to God with all my imperfections.

Though my parents experienced the Holy Spirit, our family was not a part of the Pentecostal church. In my childish ways, I believed such an occurrence could never happen to me because I was not good enough or a member of the right church. In my quest for spiritual validation, I ignored the fact that Christians in the Jesus People Movement and charismatic Christians in the Catholic Church received supernatural visitations. Because I had not encountered the Holy Spirit tangibly, I concluded God didn't care. As a logical personality more than one who relies heavily on emotions, I couldn't understand how it would happen to me, so I left the idea alone for years. Until now. I needed to have this power to witness if I hoped to marry a pastor or missionary. So, I made a vow. I told God that if He allowed me to have an authentic experience, without doubting, with the Holy Spirit, and He brought me a Christian husband, I would go anywhere, even to the mission field. I added as an afterthought—may it even be with Antti.

I made several declarations to God about my future husband. The main one was that he would be a Christian, as many unbelievers tried to date me. I also wanted him to have a suitable career, whatever that meant to a young teenage girl. A professor, I hoped, as I studied at university. Since my father was uneducated, and I didn't want someone like him, I added this to my list. My logical reasoning, based on experiences and observations, eluded me. In the natural, my desires didn't include a pastor, as I'd seen several pastors who were so poor they lived in public housing. Small immigrant churches could not pay pastors so they had to work elsewhere. Growing up in this setting led me to some negativity about the ministry.

God had heard my cries and declarations. On the last weekend of August 1972, I drove the black Chevy to the Pentecostal church camp about thirty minutes out of town, where dozens of young people gathered for their annual Youth Rally. The buildings were on the shore of a small inland lake across from a gravel road of acres of forested land. There were some buildings used for kids and youth camps. A boys' bunkhouse and a girls' dormitory came later. The church equipped the kitchen in the main building with the basics to make hot meals for participants of the various events held there throughout the summer. And, best of all, it boasted a sauna with a wood-burning stove and separate rooms for men and women, a requirement for any Finnish community since most Finns built one in their home. But a sauna by the lake with a dock and quick access to water invited kids of any ethnicity.

I scurried to complete my tasks for the day, but since I borrowed my dad's vehicle on a Friday evening, I took my sweet time after work. I enjoyed being independent of relying on rides. Once again, as I often did, I dilly-dallied around too long and ended up late.

After finding a parking spot on the grassy field, I slammed the car door shut. As I stepped out, the wind ruffled my hairdo. The culture in the sixties and seventies was for girls to wear their hair long, hanging on the side. My long dishwater blonde strands hung loose past my shoulders, though I usually wore my hair in a bun at the top of my head. Hairspray would have kept it in place, but I didn't use it, nor makeup.

It neared the end of August and temperatures lingered on the cooler side, making it necessary for warm outerwear to combat the chilly air, especially in the evening. I tossed the keys in my bag and tightened my loose jacket around the middle.

As I rushed toward the main building, I could hear the song service with the strumming of guitars. As soon as I walked into the hall, which served as the dining room and auditorium, I retreated and panicked. There appeared to be no seats available. Young people and adults occupied the benches. If only I arrived earlier, I wouldn't have to face curious eyes. I wanted to slip in unseen, but it seemed like everyone stared and made judgments. *That hair! Look what she's wearing!*

The guest speaker was a Pentecostal pastor from Finland. He sat in the front. I slipped outside and squeezed in through another door and found a space at the back. *At least I'm not the only one standing.*

If the song service lasted too long, I tended to become fidgety and my thoughts would wander. I much preferred listening to the Word and the after-service prayer time. All I desired was to be filled with the Spirit but didn't want to become a holy roller, as many were called. A put-down term I despised. Almost slander, when it was far from the truth. All I wanted was a touch of the presence of the Holy Spirit, and to accept I was worthy with power to stand up for Jesus, according to Acts 1:8. Nothing more.

After some very passionate preaching, the service officially ended. I stood near the makeshift altar near the pulpit, along with others seeking the Holy Spirit. After a while, Sanna, a friend I'd met a few years back in Toronto, approached. "Can I pray for you?"

"Yes, of course," I said.

"What would you like God to do for you?"

Here was my chance. Would God finally answer my prayer? Though I doubted at first, I surrendered to God in my mind as she prayed for me to be filled with joy. I did not reveal the real reason I needed the power, but her fervent prayer touched my heart. People who liked to pray in those days used the term "pray through." I think it means that you pray until you get an answer or at least sense God somehow. Oblivious to my surroundings and how many others sought God, I waited. We stood at the altar, but when we got tired, we kneeled. And later I sat on the floor with my legs curled underneath me. For hours, it seemed.

We all made joyful noises as the Bible tells us we should, and God's presence swooped down so thick, I sensed a soft perfumy mist in the air. I had never experienced such peace and joy at the same time. My cup filled with joy as I spoke about God's love at great length, including a few phrases in a heavenly language. Some others also spoke in "other tongues" and rejoiced. God answered my prayer.

God used Sanna and many others to "help" those who still sought the filling that night. "How was it?" she asked afterward.

"I have such joy in my heart. I've had some emotional experiences before, but compared to them, this felt different."

"How?"

"I don't know if I ever told you, but I've waited for an experience like this for five years. I even envied other Christians who seemed so free."

"Thank God."

"I understand it's not only about the heavenly language but about the power to be witnesses wherever we are in the world." I defended this but couldn't remember other Scriptures to back up my viewpoint.

"Yes."

We walked out of the building into the dark night, laughing and giggling as if we'd had too much to drink. Sanna had arrived with other girls who were from out of town so I asked her if she wanted to ride home with me. "You can stay at my house for the night. I can drive you back here in the morning."

"I would love that," Sanna said. "I'll get my things."

"Okay."

While she walked to a car on the other side of the road, I spotted my brother looking bewildered, as if unsure of where his friends were. Since a few stragglers remained in the yard, he asked me if I had seen them. No, I had not. "Why don't you look in the sauna?" When he didn't make a move, I felt I needed to help him.

Moonlight would have helped me see better. I stumbled on a rock near the shore. In a loud voice, I called out, "Osmo is leaving. Anyone in his ride, come now." I kept my focus on the uneven ground as I walked. The lights were on in the sauna and no one had fallen into the lake, I presumed—at least I heard no splashing.

I yelled again to anyone who would listen, "Anyone out there?" A guy in his swimming trunks opened the door, appearing focused on the lake, and he bolted to the dock and dove into the dark water. My poor brother. Why hadn't he kept track of his friends? His Oldsmobile remained parked on the grass in the middle of the yard. I was sure they'd find each other eventually.

I called out to Osmo, "Go find your riders yourself!" and walked back to the main building where some girls chatted.

Soon, Sanna appeared at the door carrying her overnight bag with a cheerful grin on her face. "I'm ready."

"My brother got filled with the Holy Spirit tonight."

"Thank You, Jesus. What a night!" Sanna said.

We talked and talked until morning hours. So much to share as friends with a common goal—God's goodness and boys, of course.

19

an unexpected decision

MY WORK RESPONSIBILITIES at my summer job
became more difficult after the weekend experience, however,
something happened that I didn't expect. A Christian guy asked
me for a date. The Youth Rally, a gathering of young people
from the Finnish Pentecostal churches from Toronto, Sudbury,
Sault Ste. Marie, and Thunder Bay took place at the end of
August and brought an opportunity for youth from different
cities to meet.

Local guys considered me more like a sister than someone
they would date. Of course, I wasn't available, and it was too
late. I had a boyfriend, though only through correspondence,
which made him invisible, but closer friends and our church

people were aware. Young adults from other churches, in town or from out of town, did not know of my personal life. Would I have gone out if I weren't already seeing someone? Perhaps, but my commitment to Antti remained serious. I was loyal to a tee, but also so crazy in love that my eyes could see no one else. I did, however, accept a ride to Southern Ontario from two handsome engineering students whom I kept awake through my constant chatter, although they mostly ignored me and let me float in my bliss of exuberance.

After the summer, my letters became increasingly nostalgic, yet reality set in as soon as I arrived back at university. An unforgettable summer that changed everything. Antti filled my mind all the time, and mixed feelings crossed my brain. I missed him terribly and could hardly bear the uncertainty the future would hold. *Would he come back to me?* The distance across the ocean created tremendous obstacles, but the fear that dug into my heart would not let go. I felt like I was on overdrive about when, if ever, we would be together again. We confessed our love to each other, but that's all we had committed to.

Back in London, my thoughts were of the days we spent together as a couple while also looking ahead in anticipation. What would our next step be now that romantic love surprised us? Would patience and long-suffering deepen our relationship? Or would romance fade away like the colors of the rainbow in the sky?

Often our letter conversations harmonized on topics even without knowing what the other person had written. Other times, we expressed different convictions. "Marriage is still so far away as is the possibility of it, so it seems better not to talk about it." Antti had more experience in waiting.

"Yes, I'm a little different and want to have some plans, but since we have no possibility now, let's leave it."

"Love is patient and can wait," Antti wrote.

"I surprise myself that I'm ready to marry you so soon," I wrote back.

Our dating life in Thunder Bay may have seemed different in that we often prayed together. But like many other couples, we held hands everywhere. "Guess how I remember you?" Antti asked.

"How?"

"Whenever we walked, you always wanted to put your hand in my hand differently. You put your left thumb on top, while I place my hands the opposite way. So now every time I cross my hands to pray, I put them the same way as you, so I'm there with you in thought. Just funny."

"Oh. That's different."

"I'm still waiting for your portrait. I keep looking at the photos we took, but I'm looking forward to your photo so I can nail it on the wall beside me."

I finally found a studio after procrastinating about it. "It's coming. I didn't wear my glasses, so I hope it's okay."

"Of course. At least you won't look like a fifteen-year-old. You need to do whatever you like best."

Since I revealed my dream of becoming a teacher, Antti assured me he loved me and my future career. He retreated from his own dreams of a nurse as a wife, who would be suitable in the mission field.

Often when we needed encouragement, a letter would arrive at exactly the right moment. The enemy would work on our minds with restlessness or impatience. Our love was tested repeatedly, often when we least expected it. Though we didn't argue, we disagreed about some areas, and it became clear how different we were.

Earlier, Antti envisioned his wife should be like him. Simple and normal in dress and mostly in everything else. His father instilled in him to be content with a simple life and to be grateful no matter the situation. I spent most of my earned money on myself during my teenage years. Self-absorbed. I liked clothes, shoes, and stuff.

"I don't want arguments in our future home, but we don't need to think about it now. And yes, I have firm principles, unbending, depending on the issue, but I don't dictate where the furniture sits. I'm not the bossy type."

Little did he realize my personality type. Behaviors and disagreements often show up when a couple spends time together, but we were apart mostly. He avoided conflict like the plague. His last argument with someone was four years prior! Good thing he wasn't aware of the arguments I'd had with my father, and I kept it that way.

He often spoke about our future together and his focus on ministry, which I feared would bring financial problems. And lots of debt if I continued to study for three more years. "It might not be a bad idea to be married while you finish your education. I'd have to find a secular job to earn money if we chose to live in Canada, but if we're in Finland, I could accept a pastorate position."

"That makes little sense. I can't study there. I have to graduate from a Canadian university if I'm going to teach."

The guy didn't give up easily and continued to pursue me with unanswerable questions. Would we get married with so many obstacles in the way? But we continued our "conversation" through copious writing.

Antti presented me with a serious question that needed an honest answer. "If I stayed in Finland as a pastor and never left for the mission field—this is also a possibility. Would you come to Finland for the rest of your life? Or what would you do?"

Antti mulled over this scenario while I asked a similar question of myself. "Sometimes I fear that if you wanted to establish our home in Finland, what choice would I have? I have to confess I would be against it at first, but I'm sure I could get used to it if it was God's will."

I missed him so much that it was hard to concentrate on my schoolwork. Every time I sat down to study, my mind wandered to Antti and what he might be doing. As weeks lumbered by, our plans cluttered my mind more and more. Though I attended Intervarsity Christian Club meetings, where I met other Christians, I was conflicted about my personal situation with my boyfriend.

In my second year, I lived with a roommate in a two-bedroom basement apartment closer to the university. Rebecca, a third-year math student from Hong Kong, accepted my Finnish decorations. Some long handmade rugs and a bright red woolen wall hanging reminded me of home.

The first month, I tried to settle into a new schedule with my classes and to connect with other Christian students. Since I had experienced a milestone event in my spiritual life, I evangelized Rebecca by sharing my God story of how Jesus filled me with joy. She didn't go to church or attend any of the Christian club meetings on campus, but when she had struggles, she asked me questions about God. I also met many Christian students who became my little fellowship group on and off campus. Despite how much I missed my boyfriend, my second year started off with the excitement of connecting with other Christians, although I didn't enjoy my classes as much as the first year and failed an economics test for the first time. Something bothered me. I turned to prayer, asking God to show me.

Then, a few months later, I made a shocking decision. I withdrew from university without talking to anyone. Not even Antti.

On the evening of November 9, 1972, I composed a letter to Antti explaining what happened. I'd contemplated my studies and visited the registrar's office to confirm my academic standing at the university. Once I wrote my story on paper, it released my burden to some degree. Since he wouldn't receive my letter for a week, and I couldn't hold the secret that long, I made a surprise phone call to his college.

He would be in the common area, where students gathered in the evenings. I needed to warn him about the next letter. Guilt plagued me for not talking to him about my recent struggles regarding my educational goals. Since I had never called the college before, I imagined he would be called to the phone, as it was an international call. I didn't even think how it might shock him. Or surprise him. I just worried how much my news might upset him. Would he remain steadfast or flip out on me?

I found a spot on the couch in our cozy living room and faced the bookshelves and dialed. With trembling fingers and shaking in the pit of my stomach, I dialed the dozen numbers, careful not to miss one, and waited. The ringing sounded different from the ringtone here in Canada. One long beep after another, like a muffled horn, rang in my ears for the longest minute until a human voice answered. When the person realized it was an overseas call, she probably walked away wondering what was going on. "Antti, there's an overseas call for you." I held the receiver with one hand and scratched my forearm with the other. I sighed and waited. *What am I going to say?*

"Hello. This is a surprise." The low masculine voice on the other end startled me at first because we had not communicated by phone much, and I almost didn't recognize his voice. In-person communication would have avoided many misunderstandings, but affordability became an issue because of the high cost of long-distance calls. But this was an emergency. A warning before he received my next letter.

Though I was alone in the apartment in the middle of the day, I whispered as if to keep a secret. After what seemed like minutes, although probably only seconds, I started. "I have some news to tell you. I quit university. Let me explain. You didn't expect this."

The inaudible murmur of people talking in the background almost muffled his voice, and he said, "I can't talk here. I'll call you back." The lobby was noisy, and he needed privacy, so he moved to the office of one of his professors to use her phone.

Fortunately, this provided more time to plan how to explain myself since I'd never given him any inkling, nor had I explained details of my educational program, partly because our academic programs had no comparisons.

During the fall semester, I had already dropped my Spanish class and filled the time slot with Urban Geography. I thought it didn't matter, or that he wouldn't understand, anyway.

"Why? What happened that you quit everything?" Antti sounded disappointed but not angry.

"Nothing happened and I like my life here in London, but somehow this seemed to be the right thing to do. I have written a detailed letter explaining it all."

"Did you pray about this decision before you made it? I wish you would have talked to me, and we could have prayed together."

"I'm sorry. Yes. I sought God in this. Wait until you get my mail. You'll understand. I needed to make this choice on my own."

"You could have shared your struggles with me before you did this." His voice sounded dejected or sad. He seemed betrayed. Was he unhappy about my dropping out or that I didn't include him in such an important decision?

I didn't care that he was a pastoral candidate and continued spouting words like a machine. Sentences just kept coming until they stopped altogether. He listened then finally interjected his thoughts. "I thought since we were serious about marriage, we would share every detail of our lives with each other."

"I—I—I know and I'm...I'm sorry. I will do that next time for sure." My voice crackled, and words seemed to stick to my throat.

I checked my watch as I squirmed on my couch. We needed to end the call that already cost more than our budgets allowed, but guilt gnawed at my insides as my eyes pooled with tears when I realized how much I disappointed Antti.

Would he understand this wasn't a decision made on a whim or impulsively? "I prayed a lot and even received confirmation. I have peace and sense a great relief."

"Well, that makes me feel better."

I'd been sitting on my legs too long so I dropped them on the floor and rocked my upper body back and forth. What a relief that I'd done the right thing. "I've got to tell you one more thing. About two weeks ago, a girl asked me why I was at school. She didn't know about my struggles, or how I asked the

Lord for answers. She confirmed that this was right for now after she heard my side of things."

After a long silence, Antti said, "I can't say anything to that except it made you think about your purpose in life."

"It was like God was asking me what I really wanted." Though I had not completely abandoned the idea of completing my education, I had to check my attitude and motives. "I sought a respectable position in society and security. If I got a professional career, it would boost my self-esteem."

So far, Antti had listened to my story but gave little input about my decision. Obviously, I had already made my choice. What could he say except to agree with me? I withdrew from school without telling him.

I stopped talking and listened. Even his breathing would assure me of his acceptance. I waited.

"Well, you've been under a lot of stress, but I wish you would have written to me about it, and I could have comforted you. Hey, my good girl, please promise me you will communicate with me about your problems next time. Promise me."

"I promise."

Antti assured me that nothing had changed between us, a comfort since I feared the worst. I admitted to seeking personal comfort outwardly without trusting God to take care of our future. *What if this becomes a deal breaker in the end?*

"Maybe I'll be able to come to Finland for Christmas, instead of you coming here as we spoke about. I will have some refunds, and my loan payments won't start until the summer." I tried to comfort Antti.

"I would have wanted to take you in my arms to hold you tight and whisper in your ear the words, 'Don't worry for God knows everything.' And, 'I love you.'"

It was near the end of the call, and I promised to write more details to continue our conversation. "Bye, my love, I love you."

Two letters crisscrossed paths 30,000 feet above the Atlantic Ocean. One to inform him about withdrawing from university. Another, a surprise that would change the trajectory of our lives. The details of my letter explained the process and the miracles I experienced leading up to the decision. How God had guided my steps and put things into perspective but also how it would work out practically.

Three separate miracles happened as confirmation that I did the right thing at the right time. One specific miracle happened at the registrar's office. The last day for withdrawals without a penalty for failure was October 6 and it was already November 8, but they released me without penalty, which meant if I applied to university anywhere else, I would not have failures on my records, only withdrawals. Then another miracle. I met a guy from the church who offered to store my stuff, including my bike, in his basement. He also offered to send them to my home address if I wanted. God's goodness overflowed as He cared for minor details of my life. The third, and most surprising, thing that happened regarding leaving London was a phone call from my father, who did not know I'd withdrawn from university. He would pay for my flight home. This unexpected gesture came with a caveat—help plan Laura's wedding!

20

the unconventional proposal

ABOUT A WEEK later, and before Antti's letter arrived, a slight melancholy set in regarding the decision I'd made to withdraw from university. Did I do the right thing? Or was it another one of my flighty decisions to quit when the going got tough? Up to this point, I'd aced most of my classes or pulled marks of distinction, but for one. Though I liked most of my business classes, economics caused me grief. Maybe I didn't like the program after all. Whatever the reason for the heaviness, change was coming.

Early one afternoon, I reached the side door to our apartment, hoping Rebecca wasn't home to see my stooped shoulders or the darkness in my eyes. She would sense something was wrong. I hadn't shared my deepest fears with her, but she understood me enough to see when something bothered me. Usually, I checked the mailbox at the front of the house before going in, but somehow, I hadn't even done that. So preoccupied with thoughts of failure and regret, I didn't even care to see if a letter had arrived.

After I drank some coffee and pulled myself together, I checked the mailbox and picked out the usual airmail envelope and quickly found a comfortable spot on the couch. I carefully opened the envelope with anticipation. Antti's letters always lifted my spirits, but this one seemed quite thick—a homemade card with a note inside. *Wonder what plan he now created?* The thin-lined paper crinkled in my hands as I flipped to the back and read the brief scribbles placed upside down on the top margins as afterthoughts. One of his longest letters. A piece of hair dropped over one eye, so I pushed it behind my ear. My eyes moistened and my mouth stretched from side to side. On the second reading, I switched to my analytical mind and read it several times. Would I overcome my problems with this marriage proposal, as he had presented several scenarios for our future life?

The paper crinkled in my sweaty hands as I folded and refolded it back into the envelope.

Santala
November 8, 1972

To My Dearest Pirkko,
…Would you become my wife? I have little to offer, only all my love. I thought about announcing our engagement at Christmas time and holding the wedding in Canada. I don't know what you're thinking. I've debated about an engagement all this fall but didn't know if you wanted that.

Have you considered when you want to get engaged? I don't want to dictate the engagement date, but because I'm the man, I'll propose to you.

With all my love forever...

Your love,

Antti

Providentially, the date coincided with my withdrawal from university. But a marriage proposal with a promise of more obstacles to consider and possibly more problems. I would be a suitable helpmate, he assured me. *Is that what I want?*

Those simple words heated my cheeks, though I expected this since we had discussed the possibility of marriage and prayed about it fervently. We were already in a serious relationship, so it wasn't a total surprise. His proposal letter accompanied a romantic card he had carefully created from photos cut from magazines. He also outlined some practical obtainable plans.

We prayed about how we could get married. The venue wasn't important to us. What city? And finally, what country? So many obstacles to work through before we could even get engaged. Where would we settle? To be fair, the official engagement should take place in one country, and then the wedding in another, in order to include our respective families.

Antti questioned my thoughts in many ways but gave some directives with rational explanations of what would work best. "We could get engaged in Finland at Christmas time when you come here and then have the wedding in Canada next July or August after my graduation and ordination ceremonies here."

"Well, that sounds okay, as long as we have the place picked out where we're going to live." There was no need to argue with the practicality of this, as his parents had already booked tickets to Toronto to visit his older brother's family following summer.

We discussed our ideas in several letters to find a solution. Does God guide you through circumstances?

"Here's one plan. I hope you pray about it. Not knowing how God will lead us yet. After my ordination, I mean."

"What's that?"

"What if I stay in Finland and accept a pastorate here? Would you come to live here for the rest of your life?"

"What a whopper! The rest of my life seems a little too final. I've considered that as a possibility, and I'm a little worried, but if we're 100 percent certain that it is God's will, I will accept it. But it would be difficult. I still want to finish my education. I can't go to university there. And another thing, it would mean I would probably have to be a stay-at-home wife or a mom."

"I'm sure you can find a job here somewhere, perhaps teaching English." Antti tried to console me, saying I didn't have to give up the idea of teaching.

"I would have to give up all my family and friends here, and my dream of a degree. How will I ever fit into the more strict and reserved culture there, especially in the church? I've worn makeup!"

"My family already accepts you and likes you based on what I've told them and how they see me react when I talk about you. I'm sure you will fit in with them. They are very simple and friendly and compassionate." Was he trying to reassure me?

"I'm a little nervous about meeting them. I'm so different and maybe too talkative, and I dress odd, compared to the Finnish styles."

"You don't have to worry. You will fit in with our family, and the guys at school are also excited to meet you. They've seen your photo on my wall and always remember to tease me."

"Well, that's nice."

"Another idea is that, after we marry, we live in Canada for the three years you need to finish your education. I think it would work if I get a secular job and learn English while you study. Then we wouldn't have as many debts. I would be okay to move there to London even though there's no Finnish language church there."

"But how would the denomination approve that? Didn't you have to work as a pastor in the church to repay your education loans? It's getting so complicated. We need a solid plan before we commit to marriage. First, what country we will live in and then, what city and what church? And how are we going to live? On love?"

"Yeah. I've been praying fervently about this. I hope you have, too."

"I have, but sometimes God's delays get me frustrated. I can't go on like this, away from you, not knowing when we can get married."

"It will work out. Don't worry. God answers when we pray."

After corresponding for two years, we had officially started dating five months earlier, when we were together in Thunder Bay. Antti had arrived for a two-month trip and the church needed help. His acceptance into the English language school had been a miracle, a program intended for immigrants, which he was not. The same thing regarding the church volunteer work. The pastor had resigned in the spring, and the church needed help. The pieces of the puzzle just fit together.

Obedience to God's call remained the most important part of our lives. We wanted to go where God would lead us.

Our relationship started as pen pals but morphed into a budding romance, full of confusion, self-made plans, and miracles of guidance. Sometimes we expressed our worries and feelings of depression, and other times, I poured my problems to Antti since there seemed little possibility we would ever come together with thousands of miles and the ocean between us. And as poor students, our dismal funds would not allow for travel. But God had a better plan!

"I'm so full of happiness. I had faith we would get married, as God had guided our lives so miraculously. Despite that, I didn't know you would ask so soon." The eight-page letter I wrote back was filled with joy and excitement.

Thunder Bay
November 16, 1972

My Darling Antti,

...I want to become your wife with my whole heart. Answer is—yes, I do! I want to be the best that I can be for you, and I don't expect you to provide or promise outward riches, and it's enough you will give your own love. The same here, Antti. I have nothing good to offer you, only tenderness and all the love that flows in my heart.

...But when I thought about my sister and her life, I cried and asked the Lord how He had led you to me though I felt inadequate to become your wife, but it's God's wonderful grace and love that reaches any pain of the heart.

I love you with all my heart forever,
Your only Pirkko

How well God had guided us together, almost miraculously, and I felt safe in His plan. We could pray through the many problems we would encounter in life. We'd each prayed separately for the best life partner, and God did not disappoint. He brought us together in such a beautiful way.

As I thought of how the Lord found us in two different continents, I shed tears of joy. How did I discern Antti was the right one? I listed a few things in my mind. He was spiritually mature and loved God and ministry. He was independent of his parents because he had lived in Sweden, which would help in our cross-cultural, cross-continent relationship. And I trusted him with my heart because I had shared personal worries with him and he always encouraged me. And he was not a loner, as he had good friends at the Bible college with whom he conferred. He was honest. Best of all, we were friends first, before we were romantically involved, and our spiritual life was compatible—we prayed, perhaps because we had many overwhelming hurdles which could otherwise destroy a relationship, especially a long-distance one. *More patience in the wait. But how long?*

21

engagement in finland

OUR DESTINY WAS set in motion when Antti asked for someone to teach him English via letters. I wrote to a girl in Finland, so I thought nothing of the situation other than another person to write to. Antti had decided not to date until the last year of seminary and would not get married before graduation, and he'd surrendered his life to God's service. Those plans would now come to pass, and my declaration for a Christian husband would also become a reality—unless one of us backed out, something I still feared if he found my reality was not what he bargained for. He viewed me as the beautiful Cinderella with the glass slipper, but when the clock struck midnight, what would happen?

I had a few encounters with unbeliever guys, but God's grace kept me safe. I could have gotten pregnant like any other teenage girl, but thankfully, God protected me. If God hadn't been with me when I wandered too close to the edge, what would have happened?

Knowing that my body was the temple of the Holy Spirit, I escaped from danger as quickly as I saw it coming, but still, some bruises marked me with unworthiness. Often my head bowed low from guilt as I thought of myself as a young, stupid teenager looking for love from the wrong guys who selfishly desired to fulfill their own needs.

Like the woman at the well, Jesus knew she sinned by her actions and lying to the Holy Spirit, yet he invited her to drink of the living water. The woman went away to witness to others about the Messiah. I couldn't shake the unworthiness that I was not good enough to marry a pastor or a missionary. Or to become a partner with him in the ministry. I sensed that things moved too quickly for me to process. Was I even cut out for the role that was expected of me, to work alongside my future husband?

The Thunder Bay International Airport buzzed with activity that Friday afternoon, the first day of December. A little snow on the ground had not hampered our drive. After we unloaded the vehicle, my father followed close behind and bumped the back of my flight bag with his arm. At least he carried my heavy suitcase and pushed me ahead to make room for him to get through. We were on time, as the flight had not boarded yet.

I booked the overseas flight from Thunder Bay to Helsinki, Finland, with a four-hour layover in Toronto and another short one at Copenhagen. Mother walked slowly behind us as I babbled and talked about our engagement plans and the excitement of seeing my boyfriend. My father approved of Antti as a suitable suitor for his eldest daughter and gave his blessing with the words, "You can have her if you can get along with her." His sarcasm sometimes came out wrong, but he meant no harm.

"What time do you land in Helsinki?" Mom asked.

"It arrives there at one o'clock in the afternoon, and Antti will pick me up, and then we head to Lahti right away. He has a few days off from school," I explained and assured her I would be okay and well taken care of, even though she was not the worrying type.

After the check-in, we strolled along the hallway to find a space to say our goodbyes. Mom was quiet and Dad stood stoic in this normal stance, but the sudden grin and sparkle in his eyes spoke volumes. "Tell my greetings to Antti and his family."

"Yes. I will."

Mother moved closer and placed her hands on my shoulders and looked down a bit. "Have a wonderful trip."

"Thank you." With that, I walked through the gate into the passenger waiting area for boarding.

As soon as the passengers settled in the airplane, I pulled out his last letter, one piece of paper folded into thirds as an envelope. On one side was printed the pre-stamped airmail postage of *0.50 mm* and the *Par Avion* logo. The other side left space for the sender's address, all in Finnish and Swedish. This one was from Santala, his school.

I imagined he wrote this in a hurry, in excitement. Probably the shortest letter. His scribbles were clear enough to read but spread out, different than his normal handwriting. This was the last letter before my arrival in Finland, which I had already read, but I reread his letters multiple times. This time we wrote in Finnish, much easier for him, where he wouldn't need the dictionary. Though his Finnish language skills were excellent, sometimes I struggled to decipher his messy scrawl. I'm sure his thoughts flowed much faster than his fingers. Sometimes his words merged, or slurred into a tangled mess, especially when there were no lines to write on, like on this flimsy paper. But I understood every word and didn't mind.

Suddenly, the plane was in the air. The flight attendant appeared with her cart. "Would you like anything to drink?"

"Yes. I'll take Coke."

My neighbor, an elderly woman, ordered coffee and cookies. "Where are you going in Toronto?"

"Oh no. I'm not staying in Toronto. I have a connecting flight to Finland. I'm meeting my boyfriend there and visiting relatives." My pulse thumped to acknowledge the fact that I had a boyfriend, but I didn't tell her we were getting engaged. That could lead to a long conversation and would disrupt the head games I played.

"That's nice. Have a wonderful stay and make the best of your time there."

"I will." I'm glad she didn't press further and continued reading.

After the wait at Pearson International Airport in Toronto, I boarded the larger plane, a jumbo jet, and found the window seat where I would spend about eight hours daydreaming, writing, and reading. Of course, I needed to sleep since we boarded in the evening and would miss a day before landing in Helsinki the next afternoon.

"We will land in Helsinki in thirty minutes." The loudspeaker woke me from a deep sleep. Fellow passengers beside me and across the aisle buckled their seatbelts.

"Did you feel that?" a guy in the aisle seat asked.

I straightened in my seat. "No. I slept. What was it?"

"Turbulence, like we dropped a hundred feet."

Do I care? No. Just get me out of this airplane and into the arms of my love.

I half-jogged through the crowded airport to the waiting area, where we could finally be together after four months. Antti held a red rose and wore a smile from ear to ear as I approached him at the far end of the long hallway.

At the baggage area, he pulled me into his arms. "Why did you bring such a heavy suitcase?" As a gentleman, he picked up my suitcase, but I told him I could carry the flight bag and my purse.

"Just clothes, shoes, and a winter coat which weighs a ton."

"Oh. My sister has a coat for you if you like it."

"Okay. I forgot we talked about it. I'm sure it's okay." My almost ankle-length tweed coat might be out of place. Apparently, the weather would be warmer than usual.

Since Antti didn't own a vehicle, we took the bus from the airport to the *Asematunneli*, the train/bus station, to purchase the connecting bus tickets to Lahti. The place intrigued me, as I'd never been to an underground shopping mall before. So many specialty stores and dainty cafés drew my attention before I realized we carried my luggage.

"Do you want to stop at a jewelry store?" Antti scouted a shop near the ticket booth. "We still have time before the bus leaves. Let's just look at rings. I didn't want to buy our rings without you."

"Sure. That sounds exciting." Even though my body was jetlagged, I wanted to at least take a peek at the Finnish engagement rings. No expectations of a diamond, only the customary gold band. Though curiosity filled my mind, I added, "But I can't decide anything now. I'm so tired."

"I understand, but it doesn't hurt to look. We can go shopping in Lahti later on."

He probably just wanted to familiarize himself with what I liked before we made the final decision and get an idea of how much we could afford. My excitement for the rings drained almost as soon as we walked to the counter, but I obliged and tried to keep my eyes open. After only after a few minutes, we walked out undecided, but happy.

If anyone feared awkwardness, it soon dissipated as I walked into Antti's house full of smiling faces. His two sisters, Mom, and Dad greeted us warmly, as well as his brother and his wife, who joined us from their second-floor apartment. Almost immediately I felt at home. His youngest sister, appeared a little more serious than the older sister, who was about my age, and smiled with her full face. Antti's sister-in-law, full of life, spread her one-liners, which released any tension in the room. We all laughed. My kind of people, but joking aside, I sensed their father wanted to speak. He looked comfortable and talked more than anyone else. His serious demeanor captured my attention quickly. I straightened my back and listened with both ears, even though my eyelids drooped. To understand the full meaning of the conversation, I needed to focus, especially since the conversation was in a more official Finnish language. Back in Canada, the Finnish people talked in slang mixed with English. It was important to make a good first impression.

Soon we sat down to a dinner of meat and potatoes, Finnish staples that I liked. His Mom, a soft-spoken and kind woman, created an atmosphere of peace and acceptance. I discovered where Antti got his infectious smile from. Maybe I stressed about this too much, but their acceptance of me made it easy to find conversation topics, as we came from similar backgrounds in Finland. Our villages were only one hundred kilometers apart. Their family lived on a farm in Central Finland until Antti turned sixteen. My family also lived on a small farm in the same area until I was nine, when we moved to Canada.

"Where do you plan on visiting here?" His dad asked me about my family as he gazed in my direction with a serious look. "You have many relatives all over."

Though I planned to visit my grandmother on the farm where my mom grew up, I forgot to say that and chatted about all the places nearby. "My aunt and uncle are in Heinola, and then I also have another aunt and uncle in Helsinki."

"Are they from your mother's side or father's side?" his dad asked, and then started talking about their relatives in Central Finland before I even mentioned my mother's relatives who were from the same area. His sisters showed respect and allowed him to direct the conversation. We would talk with his sisters later.

"My father's." I watched his father clear the dishes from his part of the table, showing his servant attitude. He talked about his work as a carpenter and easily answered my questions about Finland. His general knowledge and conversation, as well as his organizational skills acquired from years of service as a town counselor, blessed me. His father's excellent work habits and ethics had rubbed off on his son.

After dinner, his sisters cleared the rest of the table and joined their mom in washing dishes while Antti showed me his room, where I would sleep. "Don't worry, I have a good bed on the couch," he said when I wondered why I would take his bedroom.

After a restful night's sleep, we all went to his home church, the Free Church, where I met his friends and the congregation. What amazed me about the experience there was the number of young people. And all the kids spoke Finnish, their mother tongue, nostalgic for me. The church easily accommodated 300. After the service, Antti introduced me to the pastor and his wife, who accepted me with open arms and almost congratulated us before word of our engagement became public. I observed Antti's close relationship with friends and learned that he preached there often.

Back at Antti's home, we held a conversation about clothes. "I'm going to visit my aunt Heli and ask her to buy me a pair of velvet bellbottom pants from the factory where she works. It will be much cheaper than in the stores. I rarely cared about the cost of clothes as long as they looked good. But now I need to budget."

"Yes. We don't know our future income, so it's better to start now," Antti said.

"Can we go window shopping at least?" I was in my shopping glory in Finland, where styles from Paris were available before arriving in North America. I should have told him how he dressed well and I liked his cleanliness as a man, but I didn't.

On Monday we went ring shopping in his hometown of Lahti. Before we walked into the store, we sat in his brother's car and discussed the official date of our engagement and what we should engrave inside our rings. Antti would return to school on Tuesday. "Do you want to make it official today, December 4?

"I thought we talked about waiting until December 24, or for my birthday on Christmas Day?"

"I've thought about it logically. Since you're going to visit your relatives before Christmas, then you can make the announcement and won't need to visit again, which saves time. I thought it would be nice if you wore the ring. And I want you to come to Santala for our Christmas celebrations and meet all my friends."

"That makes sense. It would save money also, in that we won't need to travel together all over Finland to tell our relatives. Of course, we would visit the ones nearby if they aren't able to make it to the engagement party. How many of your friends and relatives would come?"

"Not sure yet, since they don't even know about our engagement."

He took my right hand in his, and I leaned into his chest with more contentment than I'd ever experienced. Anything we did together increased my commitment, and I just wanted to shout it from the rooftop. Sometimes I wondered why God was so good to me. I didn't deserve this kind of love from a man. So pure and undefiled, like the love of God. Antti broke my thoughts and whispered, "I love you."

I turned and gazed into his eyes. "So glad I replied to your request for an English pen pal. I love you more than I can say."

"Me too. We should go into the jewelry store now," he said.

After some haggling and trying on unique rings, we found the most elegant ring we could afford. Similar 18-carat gold bands with diamond-shaped designs that sparkled in the light. Since we couldn't afford diamonds, the shiny glimmer satisfied my longing for sparkle. As was customary in Finland, we purchased all three matching rings at once. One for me as an engagement ring and another for him to wear, which would show he was taken. The third ring would be my wedding band, to be placed on my finger at the ceremony. How would I place the ring on his finger if he already wore it? Something to figure it. Perhaps we'd have to bend the customs.

Our excitement brought on the giggles, like teenagers in love, while the salesperson watched us put those rings onto each other's finger. Finally, when we were again alone in the Volvo, we fell into each other's arms and kissed. We were engaged, with the official announcement coming in the next week's newspapers in Finland and Canada, as well as in our denomination's publication.

Since he was to leave the next morning, that evening we shared our stories with some family and friends. After we were alone, we talked well past midnight.

"My second cousin, who's my age, has three kids already, and another one on the way. I just want to remind you I don't want kids every year. We have to wait and see where God directs us." I wanted to make sure he understood that I wasn't ready for children right away. And I debated if I should share my most intimate issues about my body. I kept things to myself and had not shared with my boyfriend, now my fiancé, about stuff he could do nothing about. The last time we shared personal issues, he expressed how much he loved me, and even more when I talked about my struggles.

After my eyelids had drooped several times, I decided I need to tell him my worries. I swallowed a few times and turned away, pretending to straighten the bedspread. "I have to ask you. How would you feel if I couldn't get pregnant?"

"Why do you ask that?"

"Because of some female health issues, although I'm not sure what it really means. I told my doctor, but he doesn't seem to be concerned. Irregular periods happen all the time, but it doesn't mean infertility." There. I'd said it. Heat rose to my neck. His arm draped over my shoulders. Good thing the light was off. Only the streetlight filtered in through the window.

"You don't have to worry. I'm sure it will be okay, and to be truthful, I've never been to any doctor. We can trust God, like in everything else, and why would we stop now? Let's not borrow worries about the future when we have enough for today." We'd just gotten engaged and would have a lot of barriers to overcome, that was for sure. God promises to be with us all the way so we can trust Him.

"I know."

"We won't think negatively and worry about the future or whether we can have kids. Even if you couldn't, which we don't know anyway, I would still marry you. You are my life. We will do things together and trust God with our future. And even if we can't have children, I'm still in love with you and will love you in sickness and in health."

Then the pendulum swung once again and separation awaited us. For a time, we cuddled in silence as the clock ticked. Then Antti lifted his arm from around my shoulder and peeked at his watch. "It's almost two o'clock and I have to catch a train early in the morning."

"I know. I'm tired."

With that, he placed his hand on the back of my head and placed his lips on mine softly, then slipped out of the room.

A satisfied breath poured out of my mouth. *I'm the luckiest girl in the world.*

22

nurturing our bond

THE WEATHER IN Finland brought out the best in me, or maybe, the worst in my character traits. A northern country, snow usually blanketed the ground, making warm winter clothes a necessity. This year was unusual with no snow and warmer temperatures. I was happy since I didn't need to wear my winter coat, which almost reached my ankles and stuck out like a sore thumb here.

His sister provided me with a shorter winter coat, so I purchased a fur hat to match the black in the checkered design.

Both his sisters, who were about my age, dressed more conservatively than I, but I wanted to fit in.

One evening before Antti left for college, before Christmas break, I asked him, "Do you want to go shopping tomorrow?" I moved closer and touched his arm. "I want to buy a dress for our engagement party."

He didn't hesitate, although I learned he didn't care for the activity. "Sure. Hopefully you find what you're looking for."

"Yes, I hope so. I'm looking for a dress like the one we discussed, as long as my eyes don't wander to all the new fashions." My indecisiveness couldn't guarantee I'd find one quickly. My unique taste for clothes pointed in many directions. He didn't know me yet.

The next morning, Antti was ready wearing a light jacket while I battled with my suitcase and its contents. I didn't want to wear the heavy coat since I would try on many outfits, and the temperature hovered around 0 degrees Celsius. He stood at the door. "Okay, let's go."

"Hold on. Sorry. I'm looking for my sweater." I raised my voice out of habit mostly, but also to make sure he heard me since the door was far away. *Hopefully he missed how loud I sometimes get when talking to my dad. His dad speaks so quietly.*

Shopping allowed us to be alone and learn about each other. We each had developed our budgeting skills as students. He would only buy what he couldn't live without. I purchased whatever my heart desired until the money ran out. When I dropped out of university, I used the refund to finance this trip. Though I contemplated how our spending habits would work in the marriage, I bought a dress that day and ignored the price. I would have to learn better budgeting skills in order to live with this man.

"I like how nicely you dress. You take care of yourself well with your small earnings," I told him once we were home.

Antti watched as I pulled my new clothes out of bags. "When I left for Bible College, my father bought me a suit that I'd need for preaching. It surprised me since, at first, he wasn't supportive of me going into ministry. I don't know why he did that, but I'm glad he at least acknowledged my desire for ministry."

I lifted the new garment out of the bag. "That was nice of him. Oh. Look. The orange will go well with my orange tights." With small blue and orange spots against a black background and short puffy sleeves, the low V-neck dress was fitted at the waist. It was flared and didn't quite reach my knees, a mini skirt.

The dilemma of the wedding dress. What did I want? Virgin territory for me. I read Nancy Drew books as a kid and some Christian novels, but dreaming of a wedding dress never interested me. My style was simplistic, with few frills and even less lace. My sister Laura had a pink long flowing dress with long sleeves. I couldn't borrow hers as I wanted a white one.

Later, when Antti's brother and his wife visited, we discussed the wedding and our unconfirmed plans and how our marriage plans would come together. The obstacles felt almost insurmountable. Mainly the cost of the wedding, as well as whether it would be in Finland or Canada. Without pondering too much about the dress, I figured it would work out.

My future sister-in-law gifted me with some nice clothes, as we were the same size. I liked her style and wondered what she thought about a wedding dress, so I asked her. "Where do you think we can look at wedding dresses? Are they many stores here in Lahti? Or should I look at stores in Helsinki? I'm sure the capital city has more."

When she didn't answer, I decided I'd be better to find one in Thunder Bay. Why would I even think of buying a dress now? Our wedding was at least seven months away, and I had no extra money since I was unemployed.

Quick-witted and funny, she often answered immediately, before I had time to think. "You could always sew one if you can't afford one." She laughed and winked in my direction. As if I had the inclination or the skills to create one. I refuted the idea. I had sewn some clothes for myself, but a wedding dress?

"Yeah. Sure!"

Our future looked like a ball of problematic yarn, tangled at all layers. If we went this way or that way, there would be difficulties. First, about the wedding and the dress. Second, which country would work best for everyone and our pocketbook? Third, where would we live? Everything seemed like one knot after another.

After our shopping trip, Antti caught the train back to Santala, an hour's ride, and I stayed with his family for a few more days and enjoyed some pleasant conversations with his father and younger sister. Antti's mother joined with a smile and a nod whenever she had moments in between Christmas preparations. His older sister, Anneli, worked as a cook at the same campus where Antti studied, so she left earlier. I sensed they liked me, and they encouraged me everything would work out according to God's plan.

I spent the remaining days helping in the kitchen, baking and decorating gingerbread cookies, something I had done before. Then my aunt picked me up to go to her apartment, where I would spend a few days before Christmas.

"I heard you were engaged," she commented as soon as we greeted each other.

So, the word had already spread before I could share my excitement and reveal my ring. I walked to the passenger side of her little car, and we drove to Heinola, thirty minutes away from Lahti.

"We talked about Christmas, but Antti couldn't wait. We got engaged as soon as I arrived, on December 4. It's better since now we don't have to keep it a secret or listen to innuendos while visiting family and friends."

"Antti is a good man, from what I've heard. I'm so happy." Aunt Heli belonged to the same denomination, and their churches were connected.

Once we arrived at her apartment and enjoyed coffee and cake, we talked about our upcoming marriage. Funny, I never thought of asking her to sew the wedding dress. An excellent seamstress, my aunt worked at a clothing factory. "Does your factory make those bellbottom jeans I see girls wearing here?"

"Yes, of course. We have a store for employees to buy at discount prices. Do you want a pair?" she asked.

"I would love to buy a pair of plum-colored velvet ones that sit low on the waist and have big flared bottoms." I enjoyed my time with Aunt Heli. She shared many stories about my dad's side of the family.

"I'm so happy for you. Antti is a good man," she assured me. "I'm going to come to your wedding. I'll have to save money now!" I always felt connected to Heli, as her joy was contagious, even though she had her share of problems with her own family. Finnish people don't show a lot of emotion and remain reserved with strangers and talk little, not offering conversation unless asked, but not Aunt Heli. She was a fun person, full of joy and exuberance for life.

She took my measurements for the jeans. Then I boarded a bus to Karstula in Central Finland, three hours away, excited to share my engagement with everyone. There I visited my mother's family farm, where Grandma lived with my aunt's family and her four children. My uncle's family also lived in the same farmhouse but in an upstairs apartment. My young cousins hardly spoke. There's always one loud one, and that person was my aunt's husband, who joked and laughed constantly, keeping us entertained.

After a few days, I took a train south and visited with another aunt and uncle. I explored the capital city while they worked. The story behind my given name comes from my aunt in Helsinki. My mother, pregnant with me when my parents married, probably hadn't given thought to names yet, so my father's sister suggested a name. "Why don't you call her Pirkko Tuulikki?" And that was how my name came to be.

I researched what my name stood for and found that Pirkko, translated as Bridget, means "power, strength, vigor, virtue, and exalted one." My shortened middle name, Tuuli, means "wind."

All of this travel across Finland kept me busy, so I didn't miss my fiancé as much, but I wrote letters to him from every place. Antti also worked a seasonal job during the holidays, which kept us apart an extra week before Christmas. "I guess we need to practice being apart since we're going to be separated for at least seven months before our wedding," I explained more to myself than anyone else. *I hope I can make it.*

I longed for him while he was away from me. Kotka, an oceanside city in southeastern Finland, had a large meat packing facility owned by the Walroos family, a Christian business. Antti and some other seminary students worked there every holiday season packing Christmas hams.

God began teaching me lessons on submission and serving Him. I pondered our future often. *Where will we live? Which side of the ocean?* If Antti even hinted at God's direction, it would help. Living in constant uncertainty caused so much anxiety. Was I not a priority to him while now in Finland since he took the extra job at a meat factory? He worked there every holiday season, so I guessed he couldn't refuse. But why now when his fiancé was in town, and he wouldn't see her for the next half year? Was it finances, loyalty, or did he follow his father's hardcore work ethic?

I loved him too much to remain in my pity party and joined the family in the kitchen for a light lunch and waited with anticipation for the Declaration of Christmas Peace that takes place on Christmas Eve at noon. Antti had arrived home for the Christmas celebrations, which were about to begin. The aroma of freshly baked rye bread filled the kitchen as we ate, mostly in silence.

On Christmas Eve, stores closed when the big clock clanged twelve times, like metal hitting on metal. The tradition is officially celebrated as an enormous event in Turku and many other cities, but most people listened to the ceremonies on the radio or television. When they announced "Peace," it really was! It seemed eerie to see streets void of cars and pedestrians. I didn't expect the streets to be completely empty, but the culture shock surprised me. The Christmas season started with the celebration of the birth of the Lord and Savior of the world, where citizens would live in peace with one another. At least that's the purpose of the declaration.

Antti's family took the peace declaration to heart, and I got to experience the most serene Christmas ever. The chaos of last Christmas with my family became a distant memory. I moved closer to my fiancé as his father read the birth of Jesus from the Bible then led the family in prayer, acknowledging God's goodness and thanking him for the grace of allowing us to celebrate Christmas together. Somehow, I became aware he had prayed for me before he even met me, which was overwhelming in a good way, a knowledge that comforted my soul. They accepted me into the family.

The one and only Christmas when I visited Antti's home gave me a perspective on the similarity of our families. We both celebrated the big event on Christmas Eve. Both our fathers read the Christmas story from the Bible after dinner, before gifts were opened, yet there were some differences. Antti's family knelt to pray together. We didn't kneel but Dad prayed. Our family, boisterous with kids hollering and enjoying new toys, sharply contrasted with his family, who displayed peace and tranquility during the Christmas festivities. All his siblings were young adults, likely the reason, but a tinge of jealousy nipped my soul.

I tried to keep my eyes closed like everyone else, but my eyelids fluttered with moisture. My heart embraced this moment as something so beautiful that I wanted it to last forever.

Finally, the opportunity came when we visited the campus at Santala in southern Finland near the city of Hanko, the place I had wanted to attend to finish high school. Thankfully, God had other plans and protected me from myself.

The temperatures between Christmas and New Year's remained above freezing, with no snow or ice. As we strolled hand in hand around the forested pathways near the Gulf of Finland and slipped onto the smooth rocks while the ocean waves lapped the shore, we reminisced about how God had directed our steps and brought us together. My thoughts filled with gratitude. If I had followed through on my plans at seventeen, I might have missed the right time to fall in love and perhaps the right man for me.

God leads us if we pray and wait patiently for His plan, a truth Antti believed while he stood by as I grew spiritually to understand God's ways. Still, much of our future remained uncertain.

23

the confession

I NEVER ENVISIONED myself as a pastor's wife and much less the partner of a missionary. If the early years of correspondence revealed any hint of a love story, perhaps the trajectory of my life would have headed somewhere else. I engaged in a busy social life with no boyfriend except for a few unsuccessful dates while writing to Antti before we officially dated. Then, at twenty-one years of age, I fell for my "student" and "confidant," a man five years older.

Throughout our correspondence, our relationship deepened, first at a platonic level as friends and then as soulmates. I shared almost everything with him, except the thing that most needed to be brought to the table now that we were engaged.

My hands sweat, and my stomach ached. I felt compelled to share my past in order to find freedom with no secrets before going into marriage with a future pastor. Six weeks had flown by so fast, and now I faced our last night before leaving Finland. *It's now or never, and whatever happens, happens.* Before midnight, I noticed it was late. Relieved everyone had already gone to bed, we tiptoed from the living room to the alcove where he slept when he was home, which now served as my sleeping quarters. We climbed on the single bed. I fidgeted and pulled my knees up on the bed and curled my arms around them. Antti remained on the edge nearby, his fingers intertwined, and his hands resting on his lap with a puzzled look.

"I have to confess something."

Why is this such a big deal? I wish I didn't have to do this. I leaned my head on my folded knees, closed my eyes, and took a deep breath. I really just wanted this moment to be over and for our conversation to be anything but this. Vulnerable thoughts muddied my thinking. *Should I or shouldn't I?*

Antti waited patiently until I finally gathered enough courage. "I eh—em I—haven't told you this, but I think you need to know before you marry me, if you still want me."

"You can share anything and my love will not change." Antti promised to love me regardless of what I'd been through, which encouraged me.

"When I was a young teenager and working during high school, an older man looked at me wrong...and...touched me inappropriately." *There, I said it!* I covered my face with my hands, heat rising to my neck. "I... I uh... I know they should have known better. This has been my secret that I never shared

185

with anyone. It wasn't as bad as it could have been. No harm done. But I... I still remember it."

I wanted to crumble onto the floor with shame but kept silent and covered my face with my hands, keeping the tears hidden. *How can he understand?* I had to verbalize this now or never, so I picked up myself and laid it all at his feet. The guilt and shame pounded at my insides, increasing my heart rate. *Why was I picked as a girl to endure this? Did I have a mark on my forehead?* When the reality of my confession smacked me, I broke down with tears. *Why me?* I had become highly vigilant in the company of men in authority. After I spilled my guts out to Antti in the dim light of his bedside lamp, I felt better but waited for the shoe to drop. It didn't.

Soon after my confession, I sensed how comfortable I had become in Antti's presence after disclosing my secret.

Antti lifted his arms around my shoulder as I rubbed my legs around my bent knees. For a long time, we sat in silence. Time seemed to stand still. I listened for his words, but instead, he tightened his hold on me and dropped his chin in my hair. "I love you." The warmth of his breath soothed. "I love you even more now that you trusted me with your secret." I slumped forward into his lap as my hair covered my face.

BACK IN CANADA, I lived at home in Thunder Bay, and the letter writing continued. And the endless days of waiting seemed to drag. Mail constantly crisscrossed the ocean. It seemed we were in sync as we wrote simultaneously about the same topics. When a letter didn't arrive as expected, I worried. If several letters arrived in the same week, I could hardly contain myself. Though we had spent a lot of time in conversation learning about one another, we still had so much ahead of us.

Busy with church activities, I shared my testimony about taking one step at a time. How one step leads to faith and we can see the next one better. Our engagement, one rung toward the goal of marriage and future ministry, proved to be a stride of faith when life still seemed problematic, with many decisions ahead. Often, we want to take multiple paces at a time, when God only asks us to take the next one. Would He show us His plan soon enough, or would we have to wait until the last minute to decide where to live? We each prayed about trusting God's guidance.

So many voices vied for my attention. Which way to go? My indecision on whether to continue my education added more stress. The question of what country we would live in was a major life choice, still unanswered.

In February, my father reached out to Antti about pioneering a recent work among some Finnish people in Sudbury. Would we move to a new city 600 miles away? He explained how I could get a job while Antti attended English language school and ministered to an emerging congregation on the weekends. A salary would be nonexistent, and we would have to live by faith. Antti had no problem with the "living by faith" part as he entered seminary without finances and experienced miracles where God supplied all his needs. My father's proposition seemed unpopular to us, so we dismissed it.

Following the Holy Spirit's guidance remained important to us, so we waited for direction. Would God close all the other doors and keep only one open? We'd tried many doors, but they seemed to close in our faces. What did God want us to do? We waited for God's plan that would accommodate each of our goals and trusted that at the right time, He would reveal it.

Our conversation about missions had been a topic that people in the church heard many times, both in Canada and in Finland. Sofia wrote to Antti and told him I had asked her to come to Ecuador with us. Antti wrote back, "Why did you ask her without talking to me first?" He seemed upset, and I didn't think it was a big deal, as she was a mutual friend, our matchmaker.

"Do you really not understand that a missionary wife will not have luxuries and will live away from family and friends for long periods of time?" Antti drilled this into my head.

"I'm sorry. I should have asked before inviting Sofia to Ecuador with us. We're not even there and may never get there." Was I ready to leave friends behind? Though I hadn't received "the call" to missions like Antti, I daydreamed of living somewhere else, and a good Christian wife would follow her husband wherever God called. I surrendered my life to God years earlier but didn't recognize what that would entail. I was about to find out.

"Sulo, the chair of the elders' board of our church and other people in the Thunder Bay church, would want us to go to Sudbury, and even the director of the Free Church of Finland was of the opinion that they would recognize your ministry in Sudbury," I wrote to Antti, trying to convince him. Aware Antti would pray about this until he sensed God's direction, I had no worries but secretly thought maybe this wasn't it, even though I tried to influence him. It was his struggle to hear from God on this issue.

"I will pray for direction. Months ago, I decided that if I received an invitation from a church here in Finland, it would be God's plan. It's risky to put out a fleece, but let's see what happens. I'm sure I'll know before graduation, anyway."

I had mixed feelings about all of this but agreed whatever decision Antti made about his ministry would be God's plan. I would follow my husband.

"I think it would be good for you to get experience in Finland since your denomination educated you, and ministry in Canada would be difficult for several reasons." What was I thinking? I didn't want to live in Finland.

Antti had no experience living in Canada and working with immigrants so I based my opinions on my own experiences, not his. I had experienced the good and the bad about the culturally and spiritually close-knit community since childhood. I desired something different, where I wouldn't feel I completely fit into the Canadian culture because my parents raised us according to their first culture, namely the cultural norms of the old country.

When my future husband moved to Canada, he would get immersed into the Finnish immigrant community. I grew up partly cross-cultural because I lived in Canada but lived and worked in a Finnish bubble. My parents, like all other immigrant parents, brought their traditions from Finland. We lived in our own world, where many of our interactions were within the Finnish lifestyle, excluding education and work. Thunder Bay had the largest population of Finnish people outside of Finland, which worked well for the many entrepreneurs who built businesses. Even my high school of 1400 students boasted a large Finnish student population, so I felt at home with my fellow students.

Where did I belong? With all these confusing thoughts, I never realized if I moved to Finland, it would again misplace me from my culture. Where did I really fit in? If only the clock would tick faster, and we could be married. But more challenges brewed in our imminent future.

24

the love of friends

I CAME HOME in the middle of January, traveling from Helsinki to Frankfurt with a few day's stopover in Toronto to visit Antti's brother's family who immigrated a few months earlier. Correspondence through mail continued once again.

Back home, my longings intensified. I missed him more and more. It seemed the wait would be too long, and my mind kept wandering to the day he would return to me.

Antti's creativity always touched my heart. He not only wrote beautiful letters showing his love, he also crafted homemade cards with romantic photos cut from magazines. Sometimes he used our own photos, but many of them had not turned out.

Thunder Bay
Monday, January 22, 1973

My Darling Antti,

Thank you, my love, for the lovely rose card. The day I returned, I wrote one job application letter, drank coffee, talked on the phone, and gave Laura a ride. As I read your words, tears almost wet my eyes. You wrote so beautifully about our moment of separation which brought it alive in my mind, and the same longing filled my heart. What a romantic card you found.

I remember my thoughts so well when I drove the streets of Thunder Bay after my trip. Though I was happy to be back home and among friends, a strange emptiness engulfed me. Like what can I do here when my fiancé is so far away? I had been used to seeing you so often for the past six weeks. It's lonely knowing life goes on, and we can't meet on the weekends or the next day. My first feelings, but I'm sure I will go on with work and busyness. We live in hope until we meet again.

Love, your bride,
Pirkko

Life trucked along in the absence of my fiancé. My priority was to find employment to support myself and plan for our future, wherever that may be. Job hunting became my daily activity until I finally found one at the Ministry of Natural Resources as a clerk typist. The salary of $104 per week excited me, but unfortunately, it would only last until March. I needed something longer than that, at least until our wedding at the end of July. Though I worried about extending my employment, it bought time to figure out what to do about my education.

Antti not only mailed a rose card on the day I left Finland but also sent a brief letter. He received the letters I had written on January 18 and 22 on January 27, and he replied the next day.

Santala
January 28, 1973

My love Pirkko,

Thanks for the two letters and card that I received yesterday. You ~~won't believe how I've waited and hoped you would send at least a card~~ *from Toronto when you visited my brother's family. If I hadn't received your letter today, I would have probably phoned your home. I already imagined you guys had been in an accident when you got a ride with Arvo.*

I rejoiced over your letter and the things you wrote about. The Bible says, "Carry each other's burdens." I want to share joys and sorrows with you. Together we can tell everything to God and wait for the answer in time.

...I worked on my thesis last week and completed twenty pages and asked God for wisdom, and He provided. Praise the Lord!

Many loving greetings,
Your Antti

After reading his beautiful letter, I received an unwanted piece of mail in a brown envelope. My heart stopped when I read the contents. The collection agency requested repayment immediately.

How was I going to solve this problem with my short-term employment status and other debts to pay? The Ontario government had reassessed my student grants for the past school year. Apparently, my father had underestimated his income and as a result, they granted me too much financial aid—$520 worth of it.

Once again, I wrote to Antti about my problems. "Antti, I'm so depressed and too tired to write. What's the right thing to do? I still want a permanent job and went to two interviews at the bank." As per my usual writing style, I continued to explain, "Sorry, love, as this letter is so mixed up and will bring you sadness. Unable to help myself, I had to share this barely comprehensible new trial. Hope you don't take it too seriously to carry my burden. I've stressed about it all evening. But let's remember God will take care of us. We need lots of faith, so let's pray."

Was this a foreboding of our financial troubles to come? As usual, devastation in my mind took over, and I stewed about the situation more than ever. How would I pay this with a wedding coming up? Antti probably wouldn't even have a job when he arrived. Since we did not have confirmation where we would start our married life—in Canada or Finland—and faced finding a place to live, it seemed a daunting task for a young girl alone. Knowing we shared many issues about our circumstances made it at least bearable.

A week after arriving in Thunder Bay from Finland, I attended the prayer meeting at the church on a Saturday evening. I usually went home immediately afterward, but not this time. One of our youth leaders invited me to their house after service to spend time with some young adults. Their house was only a short distance from the church on the same street. I enjoyed walking, so I moseyed along the narrow road relishing the warm weather, unusual for a winter evening. He and his bride had already married and had two babies, something I wouldn't be ready for so early on.

Their house had a front porch, but we never used it, so I strolled to the backyard by the long driveway, somewhat downcast. I stepped on the landing of the back stairs with a weight on my shoulders that wouldn't seem to go away. I missed my fiancé and could hardly function, especially in the evenings. *Why did I agree to come?* Each creaky step seemed to cry out to my soul with thoughts I kept to myself. I surmised my friends wouldn't understand the situation I'd put myself in. No permanent job and a university dropout!

I put on a cheerful face as I knocked on the kitchen door. The wife opened it and pulled me into an immediate hug. "Welcome," she said. Mountains of snacks and goodies sat on the kitchen table and along the counters and even a gigantic layer cake. The smell of coffee engulfed my senses as my hostess directed me to the living room. Oblivious to what was going on, I plopped myself into a soft armchair and crossed my legs to get comfortable. Several people sat around in a circle in the small room smiling, some eyeing each other. These were friends I'd known for years and hung out with. Lahja eyed me suspiciously, and I guessed they were waiting for some reaction from me. To be at a loss for words was unusual, but when I realized this gathering was for me, or more precisely for us, I gasped.

It dawned on me they sang about a little bird. *Pikku lintu laulee reimuissaan, laulelee onneaan, eihän jouda suremaan.* (The little bird sings its rhymes, songs of happiness, he has no time to mourn.) And the words of another song about a bird finding her nest popped up as well.

After the songs ended, I rubbed my chin and stared. "Sorry, you guys caught me off guard. What's this about? I'm happy and sad," I said. Befuddled, I gazed around the room for some direction. "What's going on? This is a kid's song, and my mother used to sing it."

My thoughts were of Antti. I wished he was with me because I missed him terribly as I watched the other young couples interact with one another.

"What's it feel like?" one of the church leaders questioned and smirked. His witty commentary usually held some humor, but I didn't always "get" his jokes.

"This, or what? I miss Antti so much." I'm sure my voice sounded more monotone than usual.

The gathering started with lighthearted talk about me as the brunt of the teasing, with some serious advice intertwined in between the humor. The pastor announced the purpose of this evening. "We're here for the celebration of Pirkko's new life plan, and for the funeral of a spinster." Everyone burst out in laughter, and then I realized the real reason for the spread of food and cake. Was I dense or what? I finally caught on. My engagement party, without the fiancé.

My girlfriend's husband joined in on the continuous teasing. "Pirkko loves to talk so much that others can't get a word in." Poking fun at many of my character traits didn't bother me, as I only wished for my love's presence. One trait that everyone talked about and jokingly reminded me of was my talkativeness, hence, the nickname Parrot.

Lahja gave some serious advice mixed in with everyone's banter. "Buy all your clothes before you get married." I think the hidden meaning behind that was a pastor would be poor, and I wouldn't be able to afford new ones all the time, like my present lifestyle.

"Good advice. I'll buy clothes before the wedding for sure," I said.

The evening ended in all seriousness as everyone prayed for us and our upcoming marriage. My friends blessed our life together, which made me glad everyone approved it wholeheartedly.

I made a decision that I would work on taming my tongue to be a positive support to my future husband. However, I realized I needed to take things more seriously now that I was about to marry a pastor who was much older and wiser. When I didn't know what to do or say, my constant prayer became a lifeline. *Lord, direct our life in the way we should go, provide for all our needs, and help me with my words.* Would I make this a daily practice to live by faith?

25

shocking news

MY DAY AT work was busy filing papers and answering the phone and serving the occasional forester who stumbled into the Regional Office of the Ministry of Natural Resources. This place directed all activities around the District of Thunder Bay. I learned how to use the telex machine to send and retrieve messages as well as familiarized myself with staff who handled the different aspects of forest management. When I started, all I knew about forestry was from my father's perspective. He used a chainsaw to cut trees from government land, then hauled them to the paper mill. Clearcutting was the norm, but was it a good option for the wildlife who lost their habitats?

Proficient at the typewriter and phone, sometimes the work was tedious, and other times busy, especially during the forest fire season. When I grew bored, I read brochures or wrote letters, or started one of my marathon letter-writing campaigns.

Early in February, I was excited to get home, hoping another envelope was in the mailbox or on my desk if someone picked up the mail. The clock struck four-thirty and I hooted out of the office and speed-walked to Winnipeg Avenue. When I spotted nothing in the box, my emotions sank before I flew into the kitchen. I asked Mom, "Did you get the mail today?"

"Oh, I forgot to take it to your room. Here's a letter from Antti. Seems like he was in a hurry, as the writing on the envelope is more messy than usual." Mom had picked up a pile of unsorted papers and dropped them on the table in a scrambled mess. Recently she'd been more lethargic than normal so I wasn't surprised she hadn't cleared the table. She just wasn't herself and seemed more tired than usual. Was she sick? Her mind seemed occupied by many things. My sister Laura's baby was due any day, and I'm sure it worried Mom as much as it did me. Though my mind exploded with our upcoming wedding, I cared and often prayed for my sister.

Santala
January 29, 1973

Pirkko, My Love,
*   You're probably surprised to receive another letter so soon. This may arrive before the other one because I'm going to mail it express so you know what's going on. Now it has happened—what I have waited and even feared! Pastor Jorma Kuusinen from the Kotka Free Church congregation called, and he invited me to be their youth and children's pastor. They had discussed it in the church and contacted me first, before anyone else.*

He had already phoned during the day, and when I heard he would call back in the evening, I perceived in my heart what this was about. In the past, I've sensed something ahead of time. I talked with Jorma for a long time, and he believes I'm the right person for Kotka. Before making such an important decision, I asked for a chance to pray. I always felt a spiritual connection with this pastor, and he's one of the best pastors in our denomination. Though I was unsure about children's work, as I don't even have a singing voice, I do have a love for kids' ministry. Jorma concluded he would send more information about the position. And perhaps they want me to preach there before I make my choice… I wish you were here so we could talk about this to get clearer answers.

Loving you,
Love your Antti

Without reading further, I slumped on the bed. If I were super emotional, I would have cried and blamed God for this chaos that churned my heart. *Is this real?* Finland was far from my mind as a country where we would live. What happened to the dream of Ecuador and missions? Would Antti even listen to my side of things? If he accepted this position, I might have some prestige as a pastor's wife, but nothing else. And I couldn't even finish my education. I couldn't transfer credits to Finland, but I could transfer them to any university in Canada.

Could we put our wedding plans on hold if he accepted this? My brain jumbled emotions like a mixer beating ingredients for a cake.

Was he serious? He promised himself if a church in Finland invited him, it would be a sign from God. The hairs on my skin rose, and like a bear on its hind legs, I stood up on the inside. I grabbed the letter and tossed it on the floor, then picked it up and continued reading. He asked me to pray, but I determined I would not go. The timing was all wrong and

199

contributed to the anxiety of navigating the many obstacles we already faced.

As an enticement, Antti explained how we would live in a new condo with everything supplied, including furniture, and even a nice salary. He also pointed out my promise to move wherever God directed him, but in this case, God would have to speak to me too.

After sharing all the details about the church, like the 160 kids plus hundreds of young people and volunteers, he mentioned my youthful age. Sure, I'd barely graduated from teenager to adult. My maturity would be tested by living in Finland a few years so I would get life experience before heading to the mission field. After assessing the situation, I calmed down enough to think rationally. Maybe, if it were a temporary assignment, I could manage it, and it would be a breath of fresh air to worship in a large congregation where everyone didn't know each other's business.

As a practical man and budget-minded, Antti wrote questions about the wedding and the cost if we held it in Thunder Bay. And if we were going to live in Finland, would we need to take this or that scenario into consideration? Like the airline tickets for my parents if it were in Finland, and the cost of shipping gifts if the wedding took place in Canada. Would any of my friends and family be able to attend? Or vice versa, would his family and friends attend in Canada? And would I have to pay all my student loans before moving? And was I willing to give up my education?

When faced with major life-changing decisions, I preferred to hide my head under a blanket and forget about them. Leave me be. But now my fiancé needed an answer sooner rather than later. *I have mixed feelings about this.* What if we canceled this marriage plan? Or put it on hold. But if love conquers all, then we could solve this problem amicably.

The theme of our correspondence for the previous year always landed on trusting God and that we wouldn't miss God's direction.

Often our letters discussed the same thoughts without knowing each other's opinions. The mail moved at a snail's pace across the Atlantic. I wished we lived in the same city. My six-page message outlining many suggestions about Ecuador and Sudbury, as well as personal sharing of expectations and health issues, should make him understand.

Corresponding was the pits when facing such life-changing scenarios, which easily led to misunderstandings. Writing about my feelings became a lifeline when my pulse increased and I needed an outlet. Words spilled out, unorganized, with raw emotion. Yet, my logical brain took over more often. I had written the following letter before I received his, the one about being invited to pastor in Finland.

Thunder Bay
January 31 & February 1, 1973

My Love,
…I found out that there is a government-paid English language school in Sudbury… I received a brochure from the Teacher's College in Sudbury, but I probably won't get in because they need French language in the elementary program… I'll check it out and see if they will approve a summer course in French.

…I'll tell you what my father said about the ministry in Sudbury. He said, "If Antti has the backbone to stand in place, surprises may come." Right now, there is some kind of problem that the church has been praying about. Only the men were aware of it, but everyone has been praying.

...Would you lift the small group in Sudbury to the Lord in prayer to clear the issue and turn it into thanksgiving?

...Listen, Antti, my love, my mind seems to direct you this way, but I have to admit that I would come to Finland if God so wills and leads. Logically, it would be better for you to be here to learn English and earn money for mission school.

Our lives are so different from other engaged couples. We live apart for the longest and most important time of our engagement. We can't even plan our wedding, home, and furniture, plus everything else together as others do.

I long for your letters, my love.
Remembering you with love,
Your Pirkko

Before my letter reached the outgoing post office, and three days after he informed me about his offer for a youth pastor position in Finland, Antti accepted the position. My heart beat strangely while my brain tried to make sense of this. He hadn't waited for my reply, though he asked to me pray about it. *What's the hurry?* Weren't we in this together? Gone away from my brain were the words I had etched earlier, "I'll follow you wherever you go."

As our circumstances became more complicated, visions of me as a spinster floated in my head. Why didn't we phone each other and talk things over, especially when our future was at stake? Being a tightwad would not serve well. He could have asked for help from his parents, but his pride wouldn't allow it. When he entered seminary, he informed his father not to send him any money, and besides, his dad didn't support it at first. Antti also told God if he ran out of money, it would be a sign he wasn't called to ministry.

In addition, self-doubt about my lack of life experience and worries about the demands that were about to be placed on me as a pastor's wife played with my mind. Was I qualified? It seemed God tested me. Was I really suitable for the role of a pastor's wife? Didn't I need to know my purpose too? I mulled the consequences if I submitted to this without talking about it. Wasn't I just as important in this partnership as he, regardless of his calling? Though I never bought into the feminist movement during my first university year, I wanted to be heard before we made a major decision. Would I be considered a partner in this thing called marriage? What other tribulations would come if this overseas relationship were on the verge of a breakup?

The stormy waters of the ocean raised its ugly head. The surge of waves pounded at my heart. I loved him and I knew he loved me, but this was our first major disagreement. Though I had expressed my willingness to follow my husband if he heard God's direction, the fact that he decided without waiting for my reply hurt me.

Sensing he wanted me to agree to have the ceremony in Finland brought confusion to my already messed up thoughts. The practicality of it all seemed to rule his mind, and he made his sales pitch in such a convincing way that I had no argument until my brain fog lifted, and I removed the blinders. I had my reasoning for a wedding in Canada.

Could it be that the obstacles we faced were so unsurmountable that our marriage would have to be postponed, or worst, canceled? More bumps on the road ahead.

26

our first disagreement

WEEKS LATER, ANOTHER plan emerged. A scenario out of the blue. Would I finish my education while he pastored in Finland? But three years would be too long, and what if by then he found someone else? I wasn't the jealous type, but with the ocean between us, I worried. Would I be willing to give up my dream of teaching to move to his country? Blinded by love, I was ready to let go of those plans, regardless of how I would feel in the future.

"I could work as a single pastor for a year while you study there, and then I could move to Canada. Or maybe we should marry first?" I hadn't planned on this idea, although it seemed plausible on paper, but what about practically? I would miss him too much to continue focusing on my studies. *No. This is not it.* So, the love letters continued back and forth about the wedding.

This was too important to worry about finances. So, I made a call. No one else was home, a rarity. I pulled a kitchen chair near the wall phone and dialed. After I listened for the long beeps that signified an overseas call, someone answered, "Santala." While the person paged Antti, I scraped my hand through my hair and swallowed.

Excited to hear his voice, thoughts of what could be flashed through my mind. "Hi, Antti. I just read your letter so I had to phone. We need to talk about this. The invitation to Kotka totally surprised me. And you accepted! I didn't expect that so soon. We hadn't communicated about this."

"Don't worry. It's not completed yet. Pastor Jorma Kuusinen will write an official letter from the church board explaining everything. I still have the chance to decline." Antti seemed to suggest he wasn't sure, although he had already verbally accepted the position.

"Yes, but it's a big deal. I have to make so many changes in my life. I want to finish my studies." My mouth dried up while I waited.

"And that's why I won't sign anything until you and I both know what the right thing to do is. I'm afraid that if you come here and don't complete your education, you will regret it later."

"But perhaps if we end up in Finland, we could still have the wedding here, then I could work until the end of August to earn money to pay my debts while you start your job there," I suggested.

"Sure." Then he changed the subject. "You haven't talked about the lump on your neck. I just remembered the doctor here in Finland suggested you visit your doctor in Canada. Did you talk to your doctor? What did he say?" Concern laced his voice.

"It's a branchial cleft cyst. A birth defect that will grow if it's not removed."

"Can you get the surgery soon?"

"Yes. I have it scheduled for April."

"That's good. I'm sure it will go well. Don't worry about the scar. They can fix that," he said.

"I know. I'll just cover it up with my hair, just like I do with the eczema."

"I miss you so much, but I keep busy here. I'll write soon," Antti said.

Did he understand my dilemma about living in Finland? His compassion for ministry continued, but I sensed he seemed unsure if the choice to live in Finland was right. The clock on the wall showed our time was up, as this phone call would be so expensive.

"Don't sign anything until we both know for sure. Sometimes I'm indecisive, but wait for me." I still feared he would decide alone. When I heard some noises at the front door, I knew the time had come to end the call. "I have to go. Love you. Bye."

He assured me he loved me and hung up.

Was love enough to work through the constant obstacles we faced?

Nothing is worth more than this.

About two weeks later, I received an apologetic letter about the uncertainty he felt about the position.

Though it was dated on Valentine's Day, it wasn't the typical love letter. In Finland this day was known as *ystäväpäivä* (Friend's Day).

Santala
February 14, 1973

My Darling Pirkko,
  …Walking to Metsola after our evening snack, I wished you would be here to talk about the many things together, especially the last few days. The Kotka choice may not be as clear as I thought.
  …I realized one thing. The whole time I envisioned ministry in Canada and prepared for it, I considered the possibility of remaining here if God wills. When the invite came to Kotka, my friends told me it was my place. There is no better church.
  …Now I'm mulling over if all this plus the material benefits influenced me to accept it as God's will. Therefore, I pushed the work in Canada out of my mind because of my uncertainty. I liked Thunder Bay, but there was no need for two pastors and Sudbury was so insecure.
  …I know the brothers there would want me to go there. I should have contacted them. Your father and Sulo will receive a letter from me.
  …I can't help it, but the work there is heavy on my heart right now. Every day, when I ponder the decision about Kotka, I become more unsure.
  …You can guess how humbling it would be to admit to myself and others I've made a wrong decision in life.
  …If I was wrong, I want to return to the right road, whatever the cost, even my pride!
  …Wonder what you think about what I'm writing—certain at first and then not sure.
  …What kind of man will you get?
  Longing and missing you,
  With all my love,
  Your Antti

Before I left Finland back in January, we spent as much precious time together as possible. I'm sure he was so tired when he went back to college.

One evening, a few days before my flight back to Canada, my heart sank as I watched Antti walk out of the alcove, which served as my guestroom. The small room, next to the kitchen across the hall, with only a curtain at the doorway, served as Antti's bedroom whenever he was home. It had a single 30-inch wooden bed as a daybed along the wall. A small dresser completed the furniture.

Antti slept on the living room couch while I took the alcove. With only a wall between us and a curtain as a door, we slipped in and out of the room, waking no one else in the house.

We had been engaged for four weeks and traveled together to Santala to meet his college friends and professors. Our love for one another grew stronger in those last few weeks. With the ocean between us for the next six or seven months, we cherished every moment at his home in Lahti.

That evening, though, something seemed off. After everyone had gone to bed, we stayed up late, deepening our bond and cuddling in the alcove as usual. Though we had a lot to overcome culturally, growing up in different countries, we held similar views on marriage. We would remain pure, a given we both believed in as Christians. As a result, we developed an intimate relationship at a spiritual and emotional level more than physical.

Usually, we hung out in the alcove into the morning hours, but this time he sauntered out much earlier than usual. We had not talked about anything in particular that would have upset him, at least not to my knowledge. He just slipped out without saying a word, other than goodnight, but no kiss. What had I done wrong? Was he having regrets? *What's going on?*

27

peace at last

AS WE CONTINUED to process the events of the past few months, we talked it over as if we were together in person. "Is it God's will to listen to the judgment of others, especially peers or fellow students?" I asked, not knowing how connected his seminary class members had become.

"Praying and listening to the inner voice is not the only way to know God's plan in your life. Sometimes we need to consult those who are more experienced while assessing the situation. I convinced myself Kotka was the place for me. It seemed to be the best place, and it's an honor to be the first one in our class to be invited to a pastor's position."

"I think you succumbed to the idea that you wanted job security and prestige," I reminded him, although I'm sure he already knew that.

"Perhaps we each crave security at some level, even though we are both adventurous. I moved to Canada with family and then left home to attend university to in Southwestern Ontario, a two-day drive away. And you moved to Sweden for two years."

"True. Maybe I wanted to be like everyone else here. I watched my friends get engaged and plan their weddings and buy furniture. I wanted the same thing. Not sure."

Though I didn't always realize the burden he carried about our future, sometimes heaviness filled my heart as I considered my fiancé's dilemma. So, I sent prayer requests for him to our church. My family and church members developed a liking for Antti from the summer he spent in Thunder Bay, and they prayed for him often.

"About Kotka... I can't understand how the church there didn't question how long you would be there. Didn't they know you were heading for the mission field? It makes little sense that a church would hire a full-time children's/youth pastor for a year or two," I questioned after the fact. "But you also considered a call to immigrants in Canada at the same time. Seems confusing."

How do you discern the direction for your life? It may seem confusing at first, but when the inner knowing points to another place, it's better to contemplate further. If the job seemed difficult, then could it be God's will? Not always. He will equip those He calls and supply all their needs. He won't leave us stranded without help. God has given each of us talents and gifts, and if they correspond to our passions, why wouldn't He use those to accomplish the work of the ministry?

We learn skills through training and develop the foundational gifts we're born with. The desires of the heart may also guide our destiny. If we seek God's guidance and He lays something on our heart, we should consider it God's will if circumstances line up, especially if we've received confirmation.

Antti believed this. "My gifts are not working with children as much as I enjoy counseling and teaching, so I realize this isn't my place. And peace has been missing. Now I understand you better. You quit university and labeled it as God's will, but earlier you wrote about how God led you to the university in London. So, that's confusing."

I had no problem answering this. "Yes, I believe it was God's will, and He orchestrated all of it. I had to find a direction for my studies, and I changed my program from business to social sciences. And while you were writing your proposal letter, I was withdrawing from university. A coincidence? No. God directed each of us for His purposes without our knowledge, ahead of time. Now we can choose His guidance from now on."

"See how God takes care of all the details? You can now continue your studies." Antti seemed relieved.

"I'm sure everything will fall into place in time. Especially now, since we will not live in Finland. And my credits are transferrable to any university here."

The emotional drain that accompanied most letters from January to March about which country we should settle in lifted. One issue resolved. With the decision to live in Canada, I could at least plan my education and the wedding. I wasn't ready to give up on my dream.

"Yes, now that we've established the country, we can relax. Peace at last. That's progress," I said.

"But I'm sad that you have so much on your plate to make the plans on your own."

He cared about me and our future. Much of the planning fell on my shoulders since I still needed to make plans for my education and also put together the wedding. How I wished he were here!

LAURA AND HER husband stopped by the house with their baby and stayed until almost midnight. No one else was home, as our family had gone to visit friends out of town for the weekend. While I cuddled with their sweet baby in my arms, the phone rang. "Who could that be so late?" My sister walked over to the kitchen and answered. Was it my fiancé? Must be something serious or he wouldn't phone.

"It's for you. Long distance." I grabbed the phone and returned her baby. The lady from Toronto told me that my things had not arrived at her house as planned. Most of my stuff from London was already in Thunder Bay, but a few items were sent to her house for storage. I should have sold all my university books, but as a book collector, I couldn't.

"We need to go," my sister said after I ended the phone call. As they gathered up their things and the baby, I struggled with melancholy thoughts. When would we have children? I had experienced some women's issues. My surgery for the lump on my neck was scheduled for the next month. At least April was far enough away from July to leave time for the scars to heal. Regarding our future family, we'd agreed we would wait until I finished my education, although he wished to start a family sooner.

Wedding plans seemed to mystify us. "What day? One of my friends from the college has set July 21 as their date here in Finland so we could do it the same day. What do you think?"

Antti checked with me about some details to accommodate family members or friends who might come to our wedding.

"No, we can't because Sulo will be away that weekend, and he should be there. July 28 is better for Sulo. He should be there because you lived at his house last summer. And we're all close friends."

July 28 seemed good for both of us. "And please. No kissing every time guests tap their glass with a utensil. That's not our culture here. And besides, why would we want to do it like they do on television? No. I don't want that."

"Of course. I don't want that either. It's all private."

The wedding plans gobbled up so much space on paper, forcing me to purchase new pens every few weeks as scribbled notes filled line after line with blue ink. Would he grasp the intricacies of a Canadian wedding with its kissing games and monstrous bridal parties?

My job situation changed. They extended my contract to the end of August. When my supervisor from the Human Resource Department plunked the piece of paper for my signature on my desk, I'm sure I sparkled with joy since God answered my prayers. Why? Because we were still uncertain where we would live—Thunder Bay or Sudbury—and this extension provided job security. A colleague had broken her leg and would be away at least until the end of August, just before school would start. God's timing was perfect.

Life was busy with a full-time job, babysitting, making wedding plans, and attending night classes at the university. Plans for the wedding had to be a priority also.

28

mom's secret revealed

THOUGH IT SHOULD have been an exciting time for our family, it wasn't. Mom and Dad's arguments escalated to yelling matches. One wintry morning in early March, I awoke to loud voices. My dad was upset about something serious. Though I hadn't heard the full conversation, I guessed what had happened. My palms sweat and my fingers shook as I combed my hair to get ready for work. *It can't be true.*

"What's going on with Mom?" I asked when I got to the kitchen and tried hard to keep my voice down. When no one answered, it seemed my siblings quieted down, but I wanted to teach them a lesson, even my parents. "Don't you guys know how to communicate? We should at least listen when someone talks and not all yell at the same time."

Mom hovered near the kitchen sink, her usual place, while Dad slouched on a kitchen chair, staring into space. With her back turned toward us, I realized she was near tears, but as a stoic woman, she couldn't let us see her. I didn't notice my three younger brothers in the kitchen, though I assumed they were home somewhere, either in their room or in the basement, where they tinkered with their projects.

My sister Hilla had returned home just a few days earlier. She'd been living with a family friend, a widow, because she needed a quiet place to study for her nursing program. She stomped into the kitchen and yelled, "Why is everyone screaming? I'm trying to study."

I shook my head. "Dad just found out Mom is pregnant again," I stated matter-of-factly, with resolve, a heavy feeling settling in my stomach. "We didn't know why she's been sick and tired. She wasn't her usual self. When she told Dad she'd quit her cleaning job, Dad got mad. As I understand it, she hadn't told him or anyone else about the pregnancy. All of us were clueless. It's all a surprise."

Hilla's hand fluttered to her chest and her mouth opened. After what seemed like time stood still, she blurted, "Why, that's crazy!" Then she slipped over to Mom and placed her arms around her shoulders. "Is that true?"

"Yes."

Then my eleven-year-old sister piped up, "That's so good. I'm old enough to babysit."

I had no words. My mind leapt to the financial cost and my mom's health, both physical and mental. *I'm worried. She's forty-four.* Soon, us kids retreated from the room and allowed Mom and Dad to solve their differences. Hilla and I wandered into our shared bedroom. "Where are they going to fit another baby?" I whispered to myself, more than to her. *What about my wedding?*

Almost two months later, after the birth of my baby sister, I witnessed Dad's transformation as he fell in love with his sweet baby girl and declared to anyone who would listen, "My birthday gift!" he announced joyfully. Decades earlier, I'm sure he spoke the same words about me as the firstborn on Christmas Day, "My Christmas gift."

With the arrival of my baby sister, my babysitting experience drastically increased from just having babysat occasionally for my friends and sister. Both as a new grandma and mother, Mom needed help with the baby with four other kids at home, so I traveled between my parents' house and my apartment I had rented.

With our wedding plans in full swing, I arranged a time with Mom and Dad at their kitchen table while the baby slept in her crib in their bedroom nearby. Ideas about the wedding permeated the correspondence between Antti and I, but my parents left me to plan most of it.

Dad would contribute the finances according to his budget. It was alright since were used to low-cost everything—if you don't count my spending on clothes.

"Our church renovations will be in full swing, so that's out. The basement addition will take a long time." Dad walked over to the counter to pour himself a cup of coffee.

"Okay. How about the Independent Finnish Lutheran Church? We can have the ceremony and the reception in the same place. Besides, that's how they do it in Finland." I compromised on this, knowing it made Antti happy to have a Finnish-style wedding.

Dad slurped his coffee from the saucer with a sugar cube in between his lips, then turned toward Mom. "We pay for the reception there?"

"Yah. The ladies can make *voileipä kahvit* and maybe some *pulla*." As they had no fancy wedding themselves, they would agree to a simple wedding for us with sandwiches and sweet bread. "And cake, of course." Mom always stretched the dollar while her husband did not, so I would be okay with that.

"Yes, I'll make it work and do some menu planning," I said. Mom usually avoided direct answers to questions, meaning Dad got his way in the end.

Even though we hadn't talked about it, my father wanted one more thing. "I'm going to speak at the reception and will need at least thirty minutes."

"Okay, but don't preach too long. Know when to end." That concluded the wedding planning with the parents, except for the guest list. We trimmed it down to 120 friends and family, including Antti's family from Finland and Toronto.

A FEW THOUGHTS from our letters kept us going while we longed for each other. Writing encouragement to each other often occurred simultaneously.

Santala
March 31, 1973

My Dearest Love, Pirkko,
I love you more and more every day! These words are not just cliché, but the deepest feelings of my heart this evening.
…Your letters bring me so much love and happiness as I hope mine do to you. I read your letters many times, often in bed just before falling asleep.

…God can help us, and already has, to have authentic communication. God can help us maintain connection regarding all things… We can learn to trust one another more and more… My heart overflows with gratitude… You are just the right one for me. My love deepens through this separation.

Loving you, my fiancée,
Your Antti

Throughout our separation during the engagement, our letters displayed nostalgic longing and wedding planning.

Thunder Bay
March 30, 1973

My Dearest Antti,
This evening I'm lonely for you, my darling. Life is meaningless without you, but I have the wonderful knowledge that you are very close to my heart every moment of every day. Thoughts of you fill me with joy and great expectations for the future. We have a great big wonderful God who gives us the best things in life—He gave you to me.
…It sure is a long time to be separated, and I hope we're never apart again for this long. It is difficult! Jesus is with you every moment.

Loving and missing you,
Your fiancée,
Pirkko

The stress of the wedding lifted as the day approached. We were ready without too much fuss and kept our eyes on God and each other. "Let's focus on the primary purpose of the marriage union and not the details of how many bridesmaids and groomsmen we would want." Antti reminded me about this whenever I wrote about all the decisions we needed to make. Since we were apart for most of our engagement, we focused on each other's thoughts and feelings. We connected through snail mail, unlike other engaged couples who enjoy each other's company while planning their wedding together.

With similar backgrounds, we were not used to elaborate events or expensive décor. A simple wedding was what we wanted, though we would include all our family and church friends as well as many others. As my parents agreed to pay for the reception as a luncheon type of affair, we were glad for that and kept the costs minimal. Simple flower arrangements and place settings in the church basement would make an intimate affair for our guests. I learned to practice frugal living right down to the wedding dress, borrowed from my sister-in-law in Finland. Antti promised me nothing material, only his love.

29

the wedding

ANTTI'S LAST LETTER before he left Finland was full of
information about his days of ministry working with the
crusade tent, and his passion for spreading the gospel. To the
last minute.

Pori
June 25, 1973

My Love, Pirkko,
I'm so thankful to God for everything I've experienced here, so I will
write to my honey.

…In my heart, I sense Sudbury is our place. I'm sure everything will go well if we walk in God's plan. One week left so we can talk about this together.

With all my love forever,
Your Antti

Since we wrote simultaneously and letters arrived later, I wrote my last letter knowing I would not receive a reply. Our long-distance relationship survived the confusion and uncertainties and the longing of the heart. I scribbled a few heartfelt words to Antti so he would receive it before he departed from his home. I only imagined the emotions of leaving his homeland, his parents, his siblings, and all his ministry friends. He would be leaving everyone and everything behind, not knowing when he would be back. An enormous sacrifice.

Thunder Bay
June 27, 1973

My Love Antti,
…This is my last letter. I'm writing to you before you arrive here, hoping we will never again have to be separated by this long distance. If God gives us many years by His grace, then we want to walk hand in hand wherever He leads. It's beautiful to live in the knowledge that whatever may happen, we are in His hands.

Right now, you are at your parent's home in Finland, and in the next few moments, separation will become a reality. You will leave everything behind. You cannot know if this will be the last time you close the doors of your house. But it's comforting to know your family blesses your travels and the future home we will establish together.

…Last summer, when you stepped into the plane to come to Canada, your family knew you were coming back. It's different this summer.

...My love, only six more days and you will be with me, and soon we will see each other in our future home. I will wait for you. Loving you always, my future husband.

Bless your travel. Jesus with you.

Missing you and waiting. I love you.

Your own bride-to-be,

Pirkko

My night classes ended just before Antti arrived on July 5. I rejoiced in my first class standing, which surprised me and was helpful for pursuing a geography degree. I applied to universities in both Thunder Bay and Sudbury, prepared to follow where God directed us. Both places sent acceptance letters.

When Antti arrived in Canada, we still had no confirmation of where we would live. So, we continued to pray. Then two weeks before the wedding, we visited the believers in Sudbury, who accepted us with open arms. Soon Antti accepted their invitation to minister to the small congregation. We would move there at the end of August. Both of us would be students; Antti at Cambrian College and me at Laurentian University.

Learning to trust each other through letters posed some anxiety in me, especially when discussing such an important event as marriage. When he arrived three weeks before the wedding, we made the final touches on the plans.

"Did you bring the ring?" I eyed his bags that sat in the middle of the floor in my little basement apartment. I purchased a table and four chairs, and a bed. I didn't want to furnish our future place all alone.

Antti walked over to the kitchen and placed his arms around my waist. "How could I ever forget?" His organizational skills matched any wedding planner's, as he had completed his compulsory military training. Why would I need to worry?

Since he'd only attended weddings in Finland, I lectured him about the order of the ceremony. "When the pastor gives the cue, you place the ring on my finger and then lift your hand so I can put the ring on your finger."

"But I'm already wearing the ring. How's that going to work?"

My quick answer surprised him. "Well, you will need to take it off and give it to the best man. Your brother."

A tentative smile crossed his lips as the surprise sank in. "Why? Can't we do it like in Finland?" After a few minutes, he answered his own question. "I'm in Canada now, and I will do as the Romans do when in Rome."

Satisfied with his summation, I continued, "Did you bring the dress?"

"No, remember we agreed my mother would keep it in her luggage? They won't be here until a few days before the wedding."

"Well, I sure hope it fits. I lost weight like you reminded me. It hardly fit in Finland at Christmas time when I tried it on. That's cutting it close. What if we need to alter it? Your sister-in-law was so slim."

The clouds lifted high to allow space for the sun to warm the air and provide for wedding photography at the park. The day, July 28, 1973, arrived to say goodbye to my old life as a single woman. No more longing for my loved one to arrive. He was now here as a landed immigrant. I had not seen him that morning, as he lived with his host family, the Rantas. After we married, he would move to my apartment.

The outside doors opened wide as I stepped up the concrete stairs to the lobby of the church holding my long dress and trailing veil. As the young bride, I couldn't restrain my glee as I contemplated the day and all that it meant. *Is this real? Could anything happen? I'm about to be married to the love of my life.*

This old building built by the Finns had stood the test of time on the corner of Secord and Dufferin Streets. How many times had this place occupied a nervous bride and groom whose married life began right here, years before ours? We agreed to merge our Canadian and Finnish wedding customs while respecting our Christian traditions. So, I expected my father to walk me to the altar.

Though I was unable to see what went on inside the auditorium, I imagined the procedure. The best man, the groom's brother, would find his place beside my groom in front of the altar. Then, after the guests were seated, the other two groomsmen would step into their positions. My brother, Osmo, in the middle, and the pastor's son would line up next. Then, after my three bridesmaids walked to the opposite side, the bride, me, would arrive as "The Wedding March" played.

The piano player, a young man from our congregation, nervous as he pushed the keys with such fervor, gave the cue.

We were about to start. I imagined my groom and others checking the clock on the back wall. The time had passed what we printed on the invitation card. Two o'clock. The congregation waited while piano tunes filled the church. About ten after two, the bridesmaids and I were ready in the lobby. We eyed each other. My white wedding gown with a high rounded neckline heated my skin like inside a sauna. The afternoon sun warmed the building. The girls' short-sleeved homemade dresses hung to the floor, matching the wide-brimmed blue hats each wore. I should have cut the sleeves off my dress. Luckily, it fit perfectly, since it was borrowed. No time to look back. I tried to hold the bouquet of tiny pink roses and daisies away from the others so they wouldn't get squished in the tight space. The white wicker basket of wildflowers for each girl brought in some nature. "Don't you love the fragrance of the flowers mixed with perfumes?" I tried to make small talk. "And, Anneli, just follow the others when the procession starts."

Pride filled my heart as I watched the beautiful wedding party at the altar. *Was I ready?* Lahja, my matron of honor and a close girlfriend, now beamed with happiness as she stood at the front. Both of our sisters were bridesmaids. Hilla, my sister, with her dimpled smile, spoke of joy for me. The same for the groom's sister, Anneli, who arrived from Finland on this special occasion, though I'm sure she was very nervous, as she had never experienced this custom.

Joined by my father at the back of the church, I whispered to him, "Hold your arm like this and I'll place my arm through it." At the sound of "The Wedding March," we turned around and took one step after another. "Slow down," I whispered. Dad's face beamed with pride with a controlled smile as I guided him toward the altar. He would finally get rid of his daughter and place me in the arms of my love forever, until death do us part.

Antti's eyes focused directly on me as I approached the altar. He radiated so much love I lost sight of everyone else. The widest smile spread across his handsome face and spoke volumes. He loved me unconditionally and would never let me go.

What did I ever do to deserve a love like this?

The pastor talked about the meaning of marriage, but I'm sure I heard very little until he declared us man and wife and the traditional kiss followed. It was over, but I remembered Antti's soft lips on mine as we stepped to the registration table to sign our names.

The congregation broke out in loud applause as the pastor introduced Mr. and Mrs. Rytkonen. Our marriage held the promise of many years including challenges, triumphs, and joys, as well as unexpected gifts and future uncertainties like the ones we'd experienced in our long-distance courtship. No more separations. We were together now, in sickness and in health, our forever.

30

married student residence

A MONTH AFTER the wedding, we moved to the Married Students' Residence in Sudbury, where we lived almost separate lives for the first year, though we were crazy in love. Our circumstances dictated our lifestyle during the school year. God directed us to a new city where we knew no one. So, connecting with the small group of Finnish believers became our lifeline for fellowship and ministry. Antti attended English language classes, and I studied at the university. On weekends, we did chores together and shopped. Antti pastored while I hit the books.

After three months of married life, my nights became unbearable. For someone who never worried about sleep, this was a surprise and caused us tremendous stress. It tested our love for the first time. We didn't talk to each other and silence became a friend in our little apartment for days, unless the sound of *Gilligan's Island* on television blared its tunes. Until we decided enough was enough.

My desk overflowed with papers and books. At the sound, my ears perked. It was the same distinct noise I looked forward to every evening at eleven. A key wiggled at our apartment door. Then the lock clicked. My new husband tiptoed down the short hallway into the carpeted living room, where his young wife studied. We hugged and kissed. I relaxed, but it didn't last. The twinkle in his eyes signaled me to stop working. However, I couldn't resist asking him about school. "How was your class?" Monday to Friday, he attended English language classes for immigrants at Cambrian College.

"Good," he answered in English, though we spoke Finnish at home.

"I think it makes it easier to adjust now that you've been with other new Canadians."

"I met a young Spanish-speaking man. His wife also attends Laurentian. Let's invite them over sometime."

We moved to the couch, and he slipped his arms around me. "Yes, but after my midterms and when my skin gets better," I said.

After we talked for about twenty minutes, I glanced at the clock on the wall and panicked. *Where are my mitts?* I stomped into the bedroom as fear gripped me. I pulled the bedspread and peeked under the pillows and then stormed into the bathroom.

"I need my mitts. Have you seen them?" I asked.

Our schedules collided and we saw each other for only a few precious minutes in the evenings. My timetable scheduled day classes, so when I came home after four, he had already left for school for his evening classes.

Sometimes my medical condition irritated not only my skin but also my mind, especially when I scratched my neck and arms.

After I scrambled through my dresser drawers and dressed in a nightgown, and ranted about my body, my honey looked at me with sad eyes and pointed. "Right where you left them on the chair." He noticed how stressed I became when I couldn't find something. Still, we didn't know each other very well yet.

The view from the ninth floor of the Married Students' Residence provided free lightshows at night, with dancing stars and moonlight. A romantic view for a crazy-in-love young married couple, except for my stress. However, during the daytime, moonlike jagged rock hills caused us to envision we landed on the moon. The environment with dark gray rock formations covered the landscape. In the 1970s, Sudbury, a mining town with its tall smoke-stacks, had become known for moonscape conditions with little vegetation. I often wondered what my husband thought about my problem. Being newly married, our relationship remained undeveloped in many areas. Communication was one of them. When things became serious, we didn't talk for days. Life in the fast lane of student life shadowed meaningful conversation. Thoughts about my mitts messed with my mind.

The eczema had not bothered me in years, so I buried thoughts of it. Now this experience with my skin condition hindered our intimacy as newlyweds. Many nights, I wore thick mitts to bed so as not to scratch my body. Red spots like cherries on whipped cream covered my pillow. And blotches of dark red blood streaked my arms, legs, and backside many mornings. Once they dried a bit, the skin became blotchy and flaked off like dandruff, only to return with more scratching. The university doctor provided his expertise, and I filled every prescription for different creams, even a terrible tar-smelling lotion. I also booked a cortisone injection as well.

Why me? Would it always be like this? Nothing I tried worked. Though my husband listened to my rants and watched as I put on fresh pillowcases and sheets, I wondered how he felt. I prayed for God to heal me of this ailment.

Then one weekend, we both got fed up as I wrestled with the mitts. A Scripture spoke to my husband while he prepared his message for Sunday. *"I promise that when any two of you on earth agree about something you are praying for, my Father in heaven will do it for you. Whenever two or three of you come together in my name, I am there with you."* (Matthew 18:19 CEV).

With the Bible open before us, we knelt by our bed and agreed in prayer for my healing. I forgot about it until days later, when we heard of a visiting evangelist at a nearby church. Since we were newcomers to Sudbury, we kept aware of events and attended many meetings whenever the opportunity arose.

With new insight and faith, we went to the meeting. When the evangelist made the altar call for those who needed healing to come forward, we were first in line. He prayed, but my emotional state wavered between belief and doubt. We went home a little disappointed.

We continued with life, studies, the bedtime routine of hiding my hands inside my mitts so I wouldn't scratch in my sleep. "I'll try one night without the mitts. Wouldn't that be faith?" The next morning, I woke up with fewer spots on the sheets, but red blotches still covered my skin and some dry skin flaked off when I rubbed it.

Three days later, just like Jesus arose from the grave, I hardly believed how my skin repaired itself. The dark red, streaky blotches became a lighter color. They scaled off like flakes of sliced almonds and dropped onto the bedroom carpet. The more I rubbed my arms and legs, the more fluff covered the dark carpet. We witnessed a miracle! My skin looked healed. The eczema vanished.

With the mitts tossed into the trash and the moonlight shining through the window, we snuggled on the couch, holding each other like we would never let go. "Why don't you write letters to me anymore?" I teased Annti.

"Because you're with me now forever. I will never leave you again." John Denver's "I'm Leaving on a Jet Plane" played on the radio.

"You're sure about that? I'll hold you to it. And if you do, I'll follow you and never let you go. When we're old, we can read our letters to each other." Antti turned my head and lifted my chin and our lips met.

My sixteenth birthday at home in Thunder Bay
December 25, 1966

Me leaving for Finland at age 17, June 1968

My friend and I leaving to Finland, June 1968

Me leaving for Finland at age 19, June 1970

Meeting Antti at the crusade tent for the first time, June 1970

We meet at the tent for the first time in Finland, June 1970

Antti at the Centennial Conservatory in Thunder Bay, July 1972

Our original letters, June 1970 to June 1973

Engaged. Visiting at Santala, between Christmas and New Year's 1972

Antti speaking at the tenth anniversary services in the Finnish Free Church, June 1972

Mom and I somewhere in Finland, the summer of 1970

Dad walking me down the aisle at my wedding, July 28, 1973

Wedding, July 28, 1973

Married Students' Residence, Sudbury, September 1972

Family photo at home in Thunder Bay, December 1966

Antti and I at Hillcrest Park in Thunder Bay, July 2022

ACKNOWLEDGMENTS

MY LOVING HUSBAND. A big thank you for your dedication in writing over eighty handwritten letters and the dozens of cards that filled my mailbox year after year. I'm overjoyed for your permission to publish some of them in this memoir. Thank you for reading the first rough draft and providing your approval with encouraging words. I'm grateful you believed in me. Your takeover of household chores did not go unnoticed. We're still in love after fifty-plus years of marriage, and I'm so grateful we get to do life together for decades to come.

BETA READERS. Thank you to each one for reading my rough drafts. A few mentions here. A special thank you to Carol Ford for your leadership of The Writers Guild memoir group via Zoom. This dedicated group provided so much inspiration and accountability. So grateful to each of you for your feedback during the writing process: Carol Ford, Linda Greenberg, Esther Phillips, Carol Cunningham, Janie Brooks and Lorrie Grosfield. And Penelope Childers, Lisa Enqvist and Debbie Dueck contributed helpful comments. Anita Ball, my youngest sister, provided honest feedback with provocative questions. Miriam Kemppainen, your written commentary helped so much. Thank you, everyone. If I forgot anyone, I do appreciate you very much. And many others who critiqued my blurb or cover helped me choose the best one.

WRITING MENTOR AND COACH, SUSY FLORY. A heartfelt thank you for all you've done to make my memoir a reality. I found your Facebook *Everything Memoir* group just in time to start my story. The *My One-Year Memoir 2021-2022* group was the key to getting it done with your instruction and help through the Zoom sessions.

ARC READERS. Your advanced reading and endorsements make my writing trustworthy and validated. Thank you so much for taking the time out of your busy lives.

MY EDITOR/FORMATTER JOAN ALLEY. I'm so blessed to have found you. I stressed about all the self-publishing stages, but your patience made it seamless. Thank you for your guidance in directing the tedious editing with the various language nuances I encountered. You went over and beyond duty to make my work shine with excellent formatting and lovely cover design.

PROOFREADER/EDITOR STEPHANIE NICKEL. Thank you for your keen eye to detail in wording, grammar, punctuation, and capitalization, and for pointing out areas for improvement or accuracy. Your proofreading skills and work ethic under a tight timeline came through so beautifully. I'm proud to put my book out to the world.

MY FAMILY AND FRIENDS. Life is a story. Sometimes it's a blessing to others. Thank you to my family for your willingness to share part of our family history with the world. I trust I've made you look good, yet authentic. A special tribute to our parents in heaven for creating such an interesting life story, sometimes sad but other times entertaining. And to my husband's family for showing interest in our love story. Thank you. And to my many friends, I owe you so much for enriching my life.

HEAVENLY FATHER. GIVER OF LIFE AND LOVE.

Thank you for guiding my story through the obstacles and letting it shine for your glory. Lord, I ask for your blessing on this brief peek into our lives. May it touch others with your unconditional love.

THOSE WHO PRAY.

Thank you for your prayers before and during the publication. My husband and I appreciate your prayers that our life story may influence people to seek after God. May the Lord bless all marriages, and inspire those who contemplate marriage as a lifelong commitment or those who still look for a life partner. Everything is possible with genuine faith in a God who cares.

"for god so loved the world that he gave his only begotten son, that whoever believes in him should not perish but have everlasting life."

JOHN 3:16

Made in the USA
Middletown, DE
04 September 2023

37694367R00136